Ashley Reid Alexander

STORIES OF LOST ISRAEL
IN FOLKLORE

BY

REV. JAMES A.B. HAGGART

ILLUSTRATIONS BY THE AUTHOR

COVER DESIGN BY PAUL BUNCH

PUBLISHED BY

ARTISAN SALES
P.O. BOX 1497 THOUSAND OAKS
CALIF 91360 U.S.A.

COPYRIGHT © 1981 BY ARTIS,
ALL RIGHTS RESERVEI

ISBN 0-934666-08-3
Library of Congress catalog card n.

D1212157

STORIES OF LOST ISRAEL IN FOLKLORE

By Rev. James A.B. Haggart

CONTENTS

INTRODUCTION

Children for many generations will forever be grateful to the Grimm brothers, Jacob and Wilhelm, for preserving the Fairy Stories for them to enjoy. But not only the children are grateful. Men and women of every clime and country are grateful. Except for the efforts of these two men more than 200 stories might have been lost forever to posterity. The Brothers Grimm have assured for these simple stories an important niche in our cultural and our spiritual heritage. Yes, there is a spiritual content which cannot be ignored. For many of the stories tie in very closely with the stories of the Bible. They are particularly valuable to us for their preservation of the racial heritage which reaches back to the times of Abraham, Isaac and Jacob, the Patriarchs of the Old Testament. They give evidence of the highly Christian character of the Saxon people, as these stories are saturated with Bible truths. The symbology of these tales can be compared with the highest symbols of the Bible. Indeed, many of the symbols of Revelation and Daniel are interchangeable. So immersed were the Saxon people with the Bible content that every fairy tale is flavored with the message that the Holy Word holds.

Many suppose that the Grimm Brothers were the authors of the Fairy Stories, termed "The Household Stories of the Brothers Grimm" They did not create or originate any of the stories. They merely wrote down for posterity the old folk tales that were passed on from house to house and generation to generation at family gatherings around the open hearth. Whereas we have so many means of communication today, such as radio and television, no such luxury existed in the era in which the Grimm Brothers lived. They became increasingly aware of the values of these stories, both moral and religious, and began writing them down faithfully as they heard them. They never strayed from the oral tradition. By degrees a mass of material began to be assembled, most of them from Hesse, Westphalia, and a few from the Kinzig valley. Dorothea Wild, one of six sisters living next door to Wilhelm, was an excellent story teller. And from her old nanny the stories of "Snow-White", "Little Red Riding Hood", and the "Sleeping Beauty" were gleaned. In time Dorothea and Wilhelm fell in love with each other and married. Together they made a good team for gathering the stories before they were forgotten. As the brothers wrote, "It was just the right time to preserve these fairy tales, for those who keep them in mind are getting fewer and fewer. . ."

The brothers were quite aware of the tale's magic attraction for children, but they suspicioned something in them of a far deeper value. To Jacob and Wilhelm Grimm they were a strong and vital narrative of the Anglo-Saxon half-forgotten past. They wanted to rescue this, their racial heritage. To recover these precious gems and restore them for posterity became their sacred task. Like Daniel of the Old Testament and John of the New they faithfully wrote down each story as it was told to them, not knowing the full import of it all. The preoccupation of the Grimms with folksongs and old tales was not a mere escape into a romantic past. These words were evidence of the "ancient poetry of the common people" demanding serious and sincere consideration. As they began collecting stories in Cassel in 1810, word spread of their work and people began to come from Marburg, Eschwege and other points offering stories for inclusion in two bound volumes. The first was published in 1812.

At about this time Jacob and Wilhelm had a lucky encounter with Frau Katherine Dorothea Viehmann. She had come with her children and grandchildren from Metz to live in the village of Niederzwehren, a surburb of Cassel. The author has visited this quaint house situated on the present-day Grimm Bruder Strasse, marked by an appropriate bronze plaque. To illustrate the timeliness of their work, the brothers only knew her three years before she died. A whole sheaf of fairy tales were gained by them during this time. She was a genuine story-teller. Concerning her Wilhelm wrote, "From her we got a good number of genuinely Hessian tales. . . This woman, still vigorous, and not much over fifty, is called Viehmann. She has a strong and pleasant face, and a clear sharp look in her eyes. In her youth she must have been very beautiful. She retains these old tales firmly in her mind, a gift she says, not possessed by everyone. . . She recounts her stories thoughtfully, accurately, with uncommon vividness and evident delight, first quite easily, and then, if required, over again, slowly, so that with some practice one can take them down. . . In repetition she never changes anything, and should she make a mistake, she will immediately correct it while talking. . ." The second volume of the **Nursery and Household Tales** was published in Berlin in 1814 and brought immediate fame to the Grimm Brothers.

As scholars began to read them they began to realize that in their hands was a vast reservoir of information out of the dim and distant past. Theodore Benfrey named India as the source for all the tales and the brothers Grimm were interested in these ideas. It became fashionable to speculate on their origins, with theories presented by some that they had migrated by way of Africa (perhaps Egypt) to the Mediterranean area. There may have been a grain of truth in these scholarly speculations, but it is obvious that the chief source of the tales is the Bible. There is the constantly reoccurring theme of Jacob, the patriarch of the Old Testament, who settled with his twelve sons in the land of Goshen in Egypt. Another theme that is often used is the long trek taken by the Children of Israel fleeing through "the wilderness", or the "forest" from captivity in Assur through the "Israel pass" of the Caucasian chain of mountains north and west through

4

Europe to England and northern Europe. As sons of Isaac (Saxons) they settled in Saxony, Holland, Normandy and Denmark, to finally arrive in Ireland, England and Scotland. From thence they and their influence has spread to every part of the globe, forming new nations and kingdoms wherever they went.

In their introduction to their works the two brothers referred to their gathering of folklore as the gleaning of forgotten ears of corn. Their work of gleaning has left to us a rich fund of information about our racial past, a past that is very closely related to the Bible and the promises that God made to His very special people. . ."a peculiar people," as the King James version renders it. From a close and intimate study of these stories we, too, can glean grains of truth concerning the history of the true descendants of Israel today. The studies presented in this book are intended to disclose the unmistaken identity of these chosen people of God. The writings of the Brothers Grimm began the awakening of the "Sleeping Beauty," the Israel people who have been asleep to their true origins and heritage. The children of Israel began to come fully awake thirty-three years after the printing of the Fairy Tales in Berlin with the publication of a book in London in 1845 written by a Scotsman, J. Wilson, by the title, **Our Israelitish Origin**. Since that time the sleeping Israel has become increasingly awakened to her identity and conscious of the treasure of her heritage. May this work add to the fund of knowledge which is available today concerning the awakening Israel!

"It is the glory of God to
conceal a thing: but the
honor of kings is to search
out a matter."

Proverbs 25:2

5

The lowly cottage figures prominently in the Fairy Tales. This one, situated just east of Plymouth, England, in the village of Yealmpton, was the home of Old Mother Hubbard whose "cupboard was bare" and "had so many children she didn't know what to do."

THE STORY OF SNOW WHITE

Perhaps first amongst the folklore which has captured the hearts of young and old alike is the story of "Snow-white." It is a story most of us were told in our childhood and we readily recall the ecstasy we felt as we were stirred by its imaginative happenings; its hidden mystic meaning held for us a strange fascination which we could not quite analyze.

The charm is there yet. It is a story we can never forget. It has a staying power which permeates and lingers in the mind of the hearer. What is the magic of this age-old story and the secret of its appeal? Why is it today still so universally popular?

It was the fact of its great popularity that led Walt Disney to select it for his first movie cartoon story in color, titled "Snow-white and the Seven Dwarfs," and to immortalize it forever in the hearts of millions. Not only in our land, but particularly in Europe, as well as in other lands, the moving picture continues to be a favorite.

Mankind can be particularly grateful to the two brothers, Wilhelm and Jacob Grimm, for the preservation of this tale among many others in the folklore of the early Saxon people. They have written it down for us in its pure untainted form, just as it came from the mouths of the peasantry of their native Hanau and Hesse in Germany. Working together, these two brothers have done a service to humanity which has not been fully appreciated. For hidden within the story can be found countless messages, meanings which are carried beneath the surface of the words themselves, meanings for you and me.

Within the fabric of this fanciful tale of a queen's daughter, who was turned out of her palace by a jealous stepmother and left to wander in the woods, is woven the story of the House of Israel! It is the same story told in the Book of Revelation and in II Esdras, retold in fairy-tale form. Only the symbology is changed; the message is the same. For this fairy tale does indeed carry a message, and a familiar one to those who have made a thorough study of the Bible and of the wanderings of the House of Israel.

This simple fairy tale, passed down to us from lip to lip in the fashion of ancient Israel, tells to us in vibrant imagery the adventures of a wandering Israel (Snow-white) and her migration out of Assyria across the "wilderness" of northern Europe through northern Germany and on to England. Born of the womb of Israel wisdom, it carries with it the message of the prophets of old. It is the prophecies of Isaiah, of Jeremiah, of Daniel and of John the Disciple wrapped up in one.

An early Saxon seer (a true son-of-Isaac), knowing the punishment pronounced by God upon His people, passed along to us, by word of mouth, the story of Israel and her destiny. The story delights the ears of children, yet for those "who have ears to hear and eyes to see" there is an inner and deeper meaning. This seer, whatever his name, may stand next to John the Disciple, so intimate is his theme with that of Jesus as written down by John and known as the Book of Revelation. Let us look, then, at the story and see what it holds for us today.

Most readers of the Bible are familiar with the misfortunes of the tribes of Israel, misfortunes brought down upon themselves by their own disregard of God's laws. Moses had transmitted to them a set of commandments at Mt. Sinai, a set of laws by which God wished them to live. Disobeying them, Israel was compelled to endure the seven "times" of punishment (2520 years). This period of punishment began for the House of Israel with the capture of Samaria in 721 B. C. by Tiglath-Pileser III and for the House of Judah in 604 B. C. with the capture of Jerusalem by Nebuchadnezzar and the Babylonians.

In Snow-white we recognize Israel. In Isaiah 1:18 we find a clue to the meaning of her name:

"Come now, and let us reason together, saith the Lord: though your sins be as white as snow; though they be red like crimson, they shall be as wool."

In Isaiah's 54th chapter we see Israel represented as a woman:

"Fear not; for thou shalt not be ashamed: neither be thou confounded; for thou shalt not be put to shame: for thou shalt forget the shame of thy youth . . . For the Lord hath called thee as a woman forsaken and grieved in spirit . . . For a small moment have I forsaken thee; but with great mercies will I gather thee." (Isa. 54: 4,6-7)

In the story Snow-white is a young and exceedingly beautiful princess, beautiful enough for the stepmother queen to be very jealous. The wicked queen is easily recognized as Rome,or the Roman Papacy, described in Revelation variously as "Sodom," "Egypt," and "Babylon. " (Rev. 11:8 and 14:8)

In the Bible Israel is often likened to a woman, most often by Isaiah and very definitely by Hosea (Hosea 2). In the Song of Songs we read of the yearning heart of the young maid (Israel) for the marriage day with the Lord. In Chapter 3 we read her announcement:

"I will rise now, and go about the city in the streets, and in the broad ways I will seek him whom my soul loveth: I sought him, but I found him not. The watchmen that go about the city found me [recognized me]: to whom I said, Saw ye him whom my soul loveth?" (Song of Sol. 3:2-3.)

The most positive description of Israel as a woman occurs in the 12th Chapter of Revelation:

"And there appeared a great wonder in heaven; a woman clothed with the sun, and the moon under her feet, and upon her head a crown of twelve stars." (Rev. 12:1.)

The twelve stars stand for the twelve tribes of Israel, as also they stand for the twelve signs of the zodiac, each constellation a sign for the standard of each tribe. In the sixth verse of this chapter in Revelation we have the basis of the analogy of Snow-white (Israel) wandering through the forest, having been released by the mercy of the huntsman sent by the queen to kill her:

"And the woman fled into the wilderness, where she hath a place prepared of God, that they should feed her there a thousand two hundred and threescore days." (Rev. 12:6.)

The place prepared of God was, primarily, England, and is identified in our story as the "cottage" owned by the dwarfs. The islands of Great Britain are famed for their cottages, and also linked with this land are the activities of the dwarfs and the "little people" who inhabit trees and the earth there.

"They" in the passage above quoted are synonymous with the seven dwarfs, who lived in the cottage in the woods, a refuge for Snow white. In this connection read also II Esdras 13:40-44, and also Isaiah 42:12. The "isles" of the west, or Britain, offered the wandering tribes of Israel the refuge they needed. After lengthy journeying they gradually arrived, protected by the "angel ascending from the east, having the seal of the living God: and he cried with a loud voice to the four angels, to whom it was given to hurt the earth [Rome] and the sea [her subject colonies], saying, Hurt not the earth, neither the sea, nor the trees, till we have sealed the servants of our God in their foreheads." (Rev. 7:2-3)

In the symbology used in the fairy tale the seven dwarfs are in actuality the Seven Churches. In the second and third chapters of Revelation the symbol used for the churches is the candlestick (Rev. 1:20), and the attributes of all Seven Churches are given. The ancient Saxon seer uses his "dwarfs" as symbols of the "churches" but, moreover, links them with Revelation by placing in their hands seven candlesticks, when they came home and found Snow-white asleep in their beds.

"When it was quite dark the owners of the cottage came back: they were seven dwarfs who dug and delved in the mountains for ore. They lit their seven candlesticks. . . . "

Then they looked about to see who had entered their house. The symbols here are identical! That the seven dwarfs represent the Seven Churches is unmistakable.

The first Christian church building erected in England was by the hands of Joseph of Arimathea in about the year 38 AD at Glastonbury. England was the first to recognize and adopt Christianity as its national religion. Churches sprang up all over England and Ireland and missionaries (contrary to popular belief) were sent out from England to the continent and to Iceland. Thus the Church grew and gained strength under the protection of God's angel, free from the treacherous treatment it was receiving in Jerusalem and Rome. The Church had been well established when the Israelites began to arrive in England. This period of immigration lasted many years. It did not fully end until the time of the Norman invasion in 1066 A D, although it was largely accomplished by the middle of the fifth century.

In our story we will recall that the dwarfs said to Snow-white on her arrival, "If you will take care of our house, cook, make beds, wash, sew, and knit, and if you will keep everything neat and clean, you can stay with us and want for nothing." What better description could there be of the busied activities of the children of Israel, building their new homes, tilling their fields, building their towns and villages in faraway England, and all according to God's plan! The Church and Israel had now begun to blend. The Olive tree, or Israel, and the Candlestick, or the Church, now stood as witnesses together of God's truth upon earth, as described in Revelation 11:3-4:

"And I will give power unto my two witnesses, and they shall prophesy a thousand two hundred and threescore days, clothed in sackcloth. These are the two olive trees, and the two candlesticks standing before the God of the earth."

Students of the Bible know that the two olive trees represent the two houses of Israel, the House of Judah and the House of Israel; and the two candlesticks represent that portion of the Church which shall experience the ascension in the closing days. (Rev. 11:13)

The period of mourning "in sackcloth" is also described in the story of Snow-white. The sadness of the dwarfs when they found Snow-white had succumbed to the spell of the wicked queen corresponds with this passage in Revelation. Also, their inability to revive her the third time sounds a deep tone of sadness and remorse.

In the story Snow-white succumbs three times to the wiles of the jealous queen. The queen is thrice angry when she looks into her magic mirror and discovers that Snow-white is still alive and living in the forest with the dwarfs. While the dwarfs are away at work, she comes to the cottage disguised as an old peddler-woman, and beguiles Snow-white with her show of pretty things.

Here the symbology is quite plain, alluding to the outer pomp and show of the pagàn idolatry adopted into the Roman ritual. Buying some laces, Snow-white allows the old woman to lace her up. She is laced so tightly that she falls down as though dead.

In history this episode corresponds with the sending of Theodore of Tarsus to England by Pope Vitalian in 668 A D. As Archbishop of Canterbury, Theodore brought the Church into full obedience to the Pope at Rome, and quickly evangelized the whole of England.The services were ordered to be said in Latin by Pope Vitalian and the people of England were gradually beguiled into the Roman form of worship. Israel, choked by false teachings and a display of gaudy trappings, "fell down as though dead."

On the return of the dwarfs (on the revitalizing of the Anglican Church) they were able to revive the stricken princess, loosening the laces. This awakening of Snow-white is dramatized in English history by the passage of the Acts of Reformation by Parliament and the Act of Supremacy, which made Henry VIII of England himself the head of the Church in England, rather than the Pope (1509 A D). The Acts of Reformation stopped the flow of money from the churches out of England and into the pockets of the Pope, established that problems within the Church should be settled in English courts and gave the King the power to appoint his own bishops without consulting the Pope. In 1547, under Edward VI, England became even more thoroughly Protestant and abandoned crucifixes, images and other decorations which had been imported by the Church of Rome. A new prayer book was written in English and its use was a requirement in all the churches in England.

A second time the princess is overcome by the scheming queen, whose vanity prods her to try to destroy her rival by the use of a comb. This comb, placed in her hair, alludes to a second period in English history in which Rome regained power. Of what significance is the comb in the story?

Was not the hair the source of strength, as discovered by Delilah in her scheme with the Philistines to destroy Samson? Snow-white's hair represents Israel's spiritual strength; the comb placed in the hair by the wicked queen short-circuits that strength. The comb is also associated with Spain, being an important part of the hairdress of the women in Spain. With these clues in mind, let us examine England's history as it relates to Spain and Catholicism.

In 1553 Edward VI died and his sister Mary Tudor, known as bloody Mary, took the throne. Mary was a Catholic and offered an instrument whereby the Protestants of all England suffered punishment at the hands of the Pope. Mary made Parliament agree to repeal the Act of Supremacy and England again came under the domination of the Catholics. In order to strengthen the cause of the Roman Church, she married Philip II of Spain, also a Catholic, and began changing the ritual of the Church back to the Roman pattern. Hugh Latimer, Bishop of Worcester, and Nicolas Ridley, Bishop of Rochester, were burned at the stake and many Protestants gave up their lives as martyrs to the faith. It was a period of tense religious persecution, a purge of all those who oppposed the Roman Church.

England was saved from this second malady by the death of Mary Tudor and the ascension to the throne of Elizabeth. Elizabeth defied the Pope, refused to wed Philip who sought her hand, and returned England to the full Protestant faith as quickly as possible. By the defeat of the huge Spanish Armada, sent by Philip of Spain to subdue and punish her, Queen Elizabeth was convinced that God was on her side. Under her reign England gained a national strength and a freedom of worship which she had not enjoyed for many years.

Thus, for the second time, the dwarfs (Church) are triumphant and Snow-white lives again. Happy and busy in her little cottage, she is admonished to stay strictly indoors and let no one into the cottage again. This aptly describes Britain's policy of detached aloofness from the wars and the disturbances on the Continent.

Had she heeded the warning, Snow-white might have avoided the third malady, which was more deadly than any that had preceded it. This was the "poisoned apple," for which the dwarfs could find no cure, and Snow-white was placed in a glass case as though she were dead. Long she laid in a trance, and it remained for the Prince to come and, adoringly, behold her and carry her off with him.

What was this third malady for which the dwarfs could find no cure? We get the answer by referring to Revelation 11:7:

"And when they shall have finished their testimony, the beast that ascendeth out of the bottomless pit shall make war against them, and shall overcome them, and kill them."

The death of the Witnesses parallels the death of Snow-white. In this state of death, the powers of the dwarfs (the Church) are of no avail. What Rome has been unable to accomplish by the use of the axe, and by burning the Witnesses at the stake, she now accomplished by a more cunning and deceptive means.

The jealous queen appears now in a new form, and polishes up a nice red apple to entice Snow-white. (How mindful of the apple that was offered Eve in the Garden of Eden!) Yes, she even takes a bite out of the apple herself to prove its harmlessness.

Though the apple appeared to be a good apple, it proved itself to be a poisoned apple. So do lies and deceptions take on the form of truth. Atheism puts on a new cloak, and parades within the confines of the Church, "having a form of godliness, but denying the power thereof." (II Tim. 3:5) By planned procedure, belief in the Bible, as the true and directly-inspired Word of God, is steadily undermined. Like an insidious disease germ, it worms its way inside and multiplies and spreads until the whole body is affected with its poison.

First the Old Testament fell under attack. Then Higher Criticism leveled its guns next at the New Testament. An element of doubt was thrown in first. Men were given to question the validity of the Book. The function of the Holy Spirit, the great healing power of God, fell out of style with church-going men. The prophecies of the Bible were scoffed at, ignored. Quite gradually, the Bible has been belittled as being merely a collection of old legends and fables that have little or no relation to life today. By this subtle indoctrination Christians everywhere have been discouraged from reading the Bible. It was either beyond their ken, or unworthy of intelligent consideration.

Modernism in the Church today has spread like a poison in the minds of Christians, dulling their sensitivity to the quickening power of the Holy Spirit. In this case it was the mouth that was affected and this is the means through which the deadly mouthings of modernism are propagated. The Witnesses have suffered death more effectively than when they endured martyrdom.

And so in our story, we find Snow-white lying in a glass case, beautiful but inanimate, asleep to the coming of the Prince. But the Prince does come. The Prince loves the Princess, even in her sleep. The finale of the story, which captures the heart and imagination of every child who hears it, is the wondrous love of the Prince for the Princess, and his determination to take her away in her glass case. But by a miracle, the bite of poisoned apple falls out of her mouth, and Snow-white comes to life again. They are married and live happily ever after together.

Here we see the similarity of the story with the 19th Chapter of Revelation, which describes the coming of the Prince upon a white horse, "and he that sat upon him was called Faithful and True." (Rev. 19:11) And we read there also of the rejoicing at the marriage feast:

"Alleluia: for the Lord God omnipotent [the King] reigneth. Let us be glad and rejoice, and give honour to him: for the marriage of the Lamb is come, and his wife hath made herself ready. And to her was granted that she should be arrayed in fine linen, clean and white. . . . Blessed are they which are called unto the marriage supper of the Lamb." (Rev. 19:6-9.)

The message given to us, whether it be the story of Snow-white, or Jesus' Revelation to John, is the same. We may come to several important conclusions therefore:

First, that one of the religious leaders of the tribes of Israel, while settled in Germany, framed the story of Snow-white. The purpose and the success of his endeavor have already been delineated. Secondly, that early Saxon folklore bears out the truth that Israel today is found in the Anglo-Saxon-Celtic peoples, regardless of where they may be discovered upon the face of the earth. And finally, that God moves in strange and mysterious ways His wonders to perform. He still has a gentle hand fixed upon Israel's destiny, and upon all the overcomers.

Israel is being prepared for the coming marriage ceremony, when the glorious Prince shall come and claim His bride. When that great day arrives all the world shall know about it and rejoice. May as many as possible have their marriage garments ready for the occasion so that they may enter in and enjoy it together. Then, indeed, shall the Prince and his Princess "live happily ever after!"

The historical and Biblical references to the Roman Catholic Church in this, and other stories of Lost Israel in Folklore, is not intended as an insult or attack on any individual Roman Catholic. There have been many saints among them and this is freely acknowledged. This writer has Roman Catholic friends who are faithful Christians, but not versed in the history of the Roman Church and its papal domination in countries, resulting in the death of many thousands of Protestant martyrs who suffered for their allegiance to Christ as their Vicar.

THE SLEEPING BEAUTY

The genius of the Anglo-Saxon folklore lies in the choice of symbols, a choice which, in some cases, coincides with those of the Book of Revelation and other books in the Bible. Yet it more often employs a set of symbols born of the new environment in which the children of Israel found themselves after their escape from captivity. The significant thing about these tales is that they deal with Israel after the Assyrian captivity, and their subsequent journey across northern Europe, to their final destination in Germany, Normandy, Denmark and England.

The stories which are preserved and passed on to us by the Grimm brothers are steeped in Anglo-Saxon traditions; traditions which, through these stories, can be traced back to the people of Israel of old. They are links with the line of Jacob, Isaac and with Abraham himself! They contain the same prophecy which we find in the recorded sayings of Jesus and the long line of prophets who preceded Him! Indeed, they parallel in method the teachings of Jesus, who taught invariably in parable form. The imagery is quite as captivating and the lessons to be learned are identical, as witness the wide popularity of the Saxon folkstories throughout the world today.

While many might favor the story of Snow-white and the Seven Dwarfs among the treasured tales of the past, yet the story of little Briar-rose, more widely known as the story of "Sleeping Beauty," holds a place dear to the hearts of fully as many. We have heard these tales, all of us, in our childhood, and the characters have come as vividly alive to us in our imagination as our parents or our teachers. In later years, having coped with the realities of life, its many problems and drudgeries, we are wont to turn again to these fairy tales of our childhood in search for their old enchantment.

And we are not disappointed. This time we look deep beneath the words themselves, and the symbols, to find the core, the hidden meanings laid cunningly beneath the surface. We then gain a new understanding, one that wears better for us in our later, more meditative years. We discover, moreover, an even deeper enchantment than ever laid hold of us in our childhood. For there we find God at work, weaving an intricate story, but telling us, each one, something in his heart — something special, and something soul-satisfying.

For those readers of the Bible who are alert and watchful for the establishment of God's Kingdom upon earth, there will be no need for persuasion in the elucidation of these stories. Their meaning will come to them like a homing pigeon. For those who are given to doubts or to those who do not seem to grasp the promise of the coming of the future Kingdom as a reality, it were well that they listen to the wisdom of Jesus when He said, "Verily I say unto you, Whosoever shall not receive the kingdom of God as a little child shall in no wise enter therein. " (Luke 18:17)

If the reader of these words cannot believe in the Kingdom, even as a little child, then certainly there is no way for him to enter into that Kingdom. 'Twere better for him to read the Scriptures with the same childlike belief he had in the fairy stories, recapture the ecstasy that was his when reading of the adventures of the Prince who went through all kinds of difficulties to reach and rescue his Princess.

In our examination of the story of "Snow-white" we saw how the teller of that tale wove into it the whole history of the Israel people, starting with their wanderings out of northern Persia. There is a familiar pattern in the story of Briar-rose because she is a symbol used again for Israel and the overcomers. She represents the Israel people in another aspect from that presented through Snow-white. And revealed, for those who care to see, is her time-proven characteristic of being asleep to her own identity.

The story opens with the King and the Queen wishing for a daughter. This is a familiar opening for a fairy story:

"The King and the Queen said every day, 'Ah, if we only had a child!' But they never had one. "

There is something here that has a familiar ring to the ears of those who have studied their Bibles. In this story the tale-spinner has harked back to the tents of Abraham himself. One of the familiar stories of Genesis is the promise that God made to Abraham. We read in the 13th chapter of how God spoke to Abraham and said:

"I will make thy seed as the dust of the earth: so that if a man can number the dust of the earth, then shall thy seed also be numbered." (Gen. 13:16.)

God had made Abraham this promise, yet Abraham found himself in a very strange position. His faith in God was being put to the extreme test. Sarah, his wife, was a woman of great age, and had not as yet given him a child. We read of Abraham's complaint to God in the 15th chapter:

"Lord God, what wilt thou give me, seeing I go childless. . . . Behold, to me thou hast given no seed. " Gen. 15:2-3.)

This test put upon Abraham is one of the most familiar to us, and corresponds with the opening note of our story, in which the King and the Queen find themselves in the same plight as Abraham and Sarah.

Through the voice of a "frog" the pair are told that their wish would be fulfilled. A "frog" usually betokens a "voice," alluding to the frog's loud croaking. In this story the voice of God is symbolized by the voice of a frog.

Compare the first few verses of the 21st chapter of Genesis, describing the happiness of Abraham and Sarah, with the rejoicing of the King and the Queen when they were at last given a beautiful daughter. So great was their joy that they invited the whole kingdom to share their blessings with them in a great feast. Remembering that their daughter, whom they called Briar-rose, is representative of Israel, let us continue with the story.

Not to be forgotten among the guests to be invited were the thirteen Wise Women, or Fairies, but since there were only twelve golden plates to serve them with, one of them had to stay home. Herein lies one of the most significant messages of the story.

The symbology here is quite plain. The twelve golden plates refer respectively to the twelve tribes of Israel and the positions they held both for worship and for battle. These positions are the same as the twelve positions of the constellations of the zodiac, each tribe adopting one of the twelve signs for its symbol, or standard. These were the twelve attributes which are bestowed upon Israel (or Briar-rose), and each of them a virtue by which they shall be recognized.

As an example, the House of Judah adopted the sign of Leo, or the Lion, and those of Judah used the lion upon their marching standard and upon their shields. Identity of the House of Judah can be made in modern heraldry by the presence of a lion either on the shield or upon the field of the coat-of-arms. Numerous references are made to the "lion of Judah" and the "whelps of the lion" in the Bible.

In the fifth chapter of Revelation, one of the elders said to John, "Weep not: behold the Lion of the Tribe of Judah, the Root of David, hath prevailed to open the book, and to loose the seven seals thereof." (Rev. 5:5) In this passage we have another of the names of Jesus and He is described here as the only One who was able to read the Book of Life in the hands of God, the Father. Also, as the Saviour, He is the One who, by His sacrifice, redeemed us from our sins. Jesus is called by many names throughout the Bible, but in this passage of Revelation He takes on the stature of King and Head of the House of David of the tribe of Judah, the kingly house.

Of the twelve disciples, only Jesus and Judas were of the tribe of Judah; the remainder were all of the tribe of Benjamin. Jesus selected but twelve disciples and many have wondered why he picked twelve, no more and no less. These twelve were prototypes of the tribes of Israel. The men themselves were of but two tribes, but by their number they became types for the twelve.

Jesus manifested in human form the highest type to which man can attain. He was of kingly stature and demeanor. Judas, the betrayer, demonstrated to what depths a man can fall, having given himself once into the hands of Satan. Jesus had dealt with Satan early in his training, during the forty days he spent in the wilderness, and had overcome the lure; Judas was weak and fell, finally, to the wiles of the Wicked One.

Numbers are symbols as much as words. Beyond their meaning in mathematics, they have other meanings. To us here in our story we must heed how the Saxon mystic makes use of numbers. There were thirteen Wise Women. Thirteen is the number of spiritual testing. It brings woe only to him who cannot hew the line. In Jesus we have the first and the last (Alpha and Omega), the first and the thirteenth of the group dedicated to proclaiming the Gospel. All thirteen were equally tested during their time together. Jesus at all times was the Master and the example for His followers. He never quavered from the duties laid upon Him by the Father. But the twelve whom He called to minister for Him displayed a long array of human frailties; all of these Jesus foresaw and forgave, looking inwardly at their spiritual worth. He was looking at their souls. Judas alone failed Him in the final test.

Jesus, as the first and the thirteenth member of the holy band, was the victor in the great test laid upon Him by the Father; hence His right to open the seals in the Book and peer into the future. Judas, also of the House of Judah, was the weak member, the one who failed and went down under the supreme test. He feigned a love for the Master, a love which he did not have, and, in failing his Master, he failed himself.

To return to our story, in the twelve golden plates which the King had laid out for the twelve invited Wise Women, we see that these are the twelve positions of the twelve tribes of Israel. The thirteenth Wise Woman, or Fairy, can represent either the power of the Christ, or it can represent the power of Satan, which acts either in the individual (as in the case of the disciples) or in groups or tribes.

In the story we have an account of the triumph of Satan for a time. But that time has a definite limit, placed upon him by the Twelfth Fairy whose blessing had been interrupted. After eleven of the Wise Women had bestowed upon the Princess eleven blessings, such as, virtue, beauty, riches, etc., the thirteenth stormed into the banquet hall and pronounced her gift of doom upon the child:

"The Princess shall prick herself with a spindle on her fifteenth birthday, and die!"

But, by the clemency of the Twelfth Fairy the spell was mitigated. It was to last exactly one hundred years; no more and no less.

The spell that was cast upon little Briar-rose can be likened to the three sicknesses which overtook Snow-white, with the greater emphasis here being placed upon the third and final sickness. Struck with that malady, Snow-white fell down as though dead and nothing that the dwarfs could do would revive her. This describes the stupefying effect of Modernism within the Church today, which has succeeded in dulling the minds and spirits of believers. Working like an opiate, this scheme of Satan to pursue his machinations within the realm of the Church has succeeded to the point that the power of Christ is withheld or minimized by a lack of acceptance necessary to its fullest manifestation. This dullness of spirit is also described by Jesus in Revelation 3:16 as "luke-warmness," the belief of the churchmen of Laodicea, which is the characteristic of the seventh Church, or the church of today.

The sleep that overtook Briar-rose carries another meaning for us today. Sleep has all the qualities of death, as far as the ego, or consciousness, is concerned. The body lies inert and inactive, yet it is alive and has the potentiality of full consciousness. The "sleeping beauty," then, is sleeping Israel, who, in her state of sleep, hasn't the slightest notion as to whom she is. The people of Israel exist in the world today, yet they are unaware that they are Israel. It is a peculiar truth that their enemies know them better than they know themselves, and seek to do away with them before they awaken to their real identity.

So, as portrayed in our story, the maid and all creatures about her lay in a deep sleep. After the hundred years and only at the appointed time, would the Prince come who would awaken and liberate her.

There is some solace here for those who are impatient that the Anglo-Saxon-Celtic peoples of the world today are largely unaware that they are Israel. In our story the future of these people is hidden. Although there are some stirrings at the present time, some recognition, Israel shall not be really cognizant of her heritage until the coming of her King, the Christ, who shall ascend the Throne of David and be her ruler.

It is a touching episode that the father of Briar-rose tried to protect the child by ordering every spindle burned in order to destroy the spindle that might prick the girl and cause her to "fall down as though dead." This is the love of the Father for his daughter, Israel, portrayed so dramatically all through the Bible, with varying degrees of fatherly affection avowed. Many loud thunderings and threats are cast over the people, yet all the while He is watching over them, loving them, hoping they will avoid the blunders and mistakes which threaten to obliterate them. He would, if He could, take from them "this cup" of bitterness, of suffering, and the fate of wandering aimlessly through the wilderness, a "lost" people.

But the drama of these people is the theme of the Bible, just as it is the theme of our story, and their destiny must be fulfilled. God allows a kind of punishment to fall upon His chosen people, a chastisement from which He hopes they will emerge a stronger, more spiritual people.

The powers of Satan, operating through the vengeful feeling of the thirteenth Fairy, is given sway. But the spell laid upon Briar-rose (Israel) is for a definite length of time, beyond which she loses her power and the Princess shall awake and arise. At the end of one hundred years she was to be wakened by a kiss from the Prince. Then the whole kingdom would awaken and become aware of their true selves.

This is symbolical of the "awakening" of Israel, preparatory to her joyous entering into the glory of the Kingdom of God, which has been promised by the Prince of Peace himself so many, many times in the Scriptures. Herein lies the fulfillment of all the prophecies, of Isaiah 60:1 when he says:

"Arise, shine; for thy light is come, and the glory of the Lord is risen upon thee!"

It is the same kingdom spoken of by Daniel:

"And the stone that smote the image became a great mountain, and filled the whole earth." (Dan. 2:35.)

And in Joel 2:1 we read these words:

" Blow ye the trumpet in Zion, and sound an alarm in my holy mountain: let all the inhabitants of the land tremble: for the day of the Lord cometh, for it is nigh at hand."

Micah speaks of it in these words:

"But in the last days it shall come to pass, that the mountain of the house of the Lord shall be established in the top of the mountains, and it shall be exalted above the hills; and people shall flow unto it. . . But they shall sit every man under his vine and under his fig tree; and none shall make them afraid." (Micah 4:1-4.)

It will be remembered that after Briar-rose felt the prick of the old woman's spindle "she fell down upon a bed that stood there, and lay in a deep sleep. And this sleep extended over the whole palace. . . ." Then "there began to grow a hedge of thorns, which every year became higher, and at last grew close up around the castle and all over it, so that there was nothing of it to be seen, not even the flag upon the roof."

The flag upon the roof, of course, would carry the telling symbol that would identify the people of that kingdom. This indicates that even the name of these people was erased; they can no longer tell who they are. This part of the story indicates the complete obliteration of the identity of the ten tribes of Israel. These people, asleep to their own identity, do not of themselves have the power to wake themselves.

"From time to time, many kings' sons came and tried to get through the thorny hedge into the castle, "having heard of the beautiful princess asleep inside. These kings sons represent the martyrs of the Church, sons of the Faith, who have stood valiantly against the "thorns" of persecution and fought through the morass of superstition and false belief in a courageous attempt to rescue the Truth. Such men, down through the centuries, have witnessed the majesty of the Kingdom of Heaven and, being overwhelmed with its beauty and its glory, have sought to point out the way to the rest of their fellows. Such men have given their lives gladly, knowing the truth of their own immortality in Christ. They have striven to arouse Israel so that she might awaken to a new life, to the happy life within the Kingdom.

From Stephen, stoned at the gates of Jerusalem, to the martyrs of the present day, those hundreds of Christian missionaries caught behind the Bamboo and the Iron Curtain who have died in concentration camps or prisons, a long stream of "king's sons" have striven to break their way through the thorny wall that surrounds the castle, but without success. These men have given their lives for their faith and, according to the Bible (Revelation 21:2-4), they shall not go unrewarded.

Let us remember that, in our story, it was destined for one Prince, and one alone, to break through the hedge and awaken the sleeping Princess. Only at an exact hour, when a hundred years had passed, could this Prince break through and reach the side of his Princess.

The Bible is crammed with prophecy. Men of vision have been shown and have foretold the whole scheme of coming events. The dark future had been spelled out for Israel by the people themselves when they consciously broke the laws laid down for them at Mt. Sinai. Yet, to certain ones who remained true, God gave an insight into the glorious destiny of His people.

By reason of His great sacrifice, God gave His most detailed vision of the future to His son, Jesus Christ, written down by His disciple John and known to us as the Book of Revelation. For those who have studied closely the prophecy contained in this book, and have compared it with the words of the other great prophets who preceded him, one gains a sense of the immensity of God's plan and the definite timing of it. It is, indeed, a timetable, usable by those who have learned to read it. It was written in code, truly, but by the unfathomable power of faith and the subtle influx of the Holy Spirit of God, the true believer can comprehend this timetable and know exactly where he stands in terms of God's plan. Only Jesus Christ knows the exact hour, the proper, for the awakening, but we know that it will happen, according to His plan for us.

"The youth said, 'I am not afraid, I will go and see the beautiful Briar-rose.'" Such were the determined words of the Prince. Jesus, the Christ, never knew fear at any time in His ministry upon earth. He was, rather, the very personification of courage. His calm poise while

21

standing trial before the authorities of both Rome and Jewry, displayed a courage that comes only with a sense of oneness with the Father.

Only Jesus Christ is fully conscious of His coming role in the restoration of the Kingdom of God on earth. One by one those who are to be its citizens are brushing the sleep from their eyes and are answering to His impulsion. As it is written in the 19th chapter of Revelation:

"I saw heaven opened, and behold a white horse; and he that sat upon him was called Faithful and True, and in righteousness he doth judge and make war."

The Prince of Peace, as a gallant warrior, a knight-errant, comes riding through the mists of time. The thorned thicket parts and he rides on out to his mission. His hour has come; He has long awaited it, for in this moment he and his people are joined in a joyous reunion.

In the fairy tale, when the Prince arrived, the beautiful Princess, asleep for so long, awakened and "looked at him quite sweetly." Immediately the King and the whole court came to renewed life, even to the birds on the roof and the flies on the wall. "Then the marriage of the King's son with Briar-rose was celebrated with splendor, and they lived happily ever after."

"The marriage of the Lamb is come," it is announced in Revelation 19:7, "and his wife hath made herself ready." Again we find our Saxon folktale closely parallels the Divine theme of the Scriptures. Those who have prepared themselves (see Matthew 25:1-13) are ready to celebrate the marriage of the Christ with His people Israel.

There remains but one preliminary step, preparing the way for the full restoration of the Kingdom of God on earth. The power of "that old serpent, which is the Devil" still holds sway upon the earth, but the hour of his departure bears close upon him. We read in the 20th chapter of Revelation that "an angel came down from heaven . . . and he laid hold on the dragon, that old serpent, which is the Devil, and Satan, and bound him. . . ." Thus ends the period of control by this creature, which in our story was the "thirteenth fairy," the "one hundred years" during which the Princess slept.

At the end of the appointed time the Prince (Christ) will adventure forth and to Him will be given all power over heaven and earth. He shall be "King of kings and Lord of lords" and His bride shall join Him in the marriage which shall begin a long and happy reign.

Thus, it can be seen that the Saxon sage who composed the story of Briar-rose had a definite picture of the future which he wished to impart to his hearers. He penned the story primarily for the innocent ears of children and they have loved this story down through the centuries. But he had other things to say, things which will reveal themselves to his readers as the Marriage Day with the Lord draws closer and closer. To these his tale rings clear and true and holds several important messages.

First, and most important in this story, he predicts the sleep-consciousness which shall overcome the tribes of Israel. They shall, in this state, be unaware of their identity and their destiny. Then, in due time, they shall awaken to their responsibilities as the children of God and, by the power and very presence of the Christ, shall draw all peoples into a state of happiness and perfection that has never been known on the earth.

The judgment aspect of the Christ does not receive emphasis in this story, but rather the joy that rings out at the reunion of Israel with her Lord and Christ in the new order on the earth. Again, our author wishes us to know that God has established a pattern of perfection, which will be unfolded in due order and with a precision that we can scarcely imagine. This story seems to bid straight to our hearts and to our faith, showing that God does rule in this our universe and that we, as we respond to His way of life, shall inherit that which is truly ours in Christ.

**Dunsford, So. Devon
England**

CINDERELLA

Everyone knows the story of Cinderella. We never seem to tire of hearing about this unfortunate girl who lost her mother and how, when her father decided to marry again, she was subjected to the domination and the scorn of a stepmother and her two jealous daughters. The theme is as familiar to us as an old shoe. Of the great store of fairy tales, it is today definitely a favorite.

A testimonial to its popularity is the "Ella Cinders" comic strip which has appeared in newspapers throughout the country for years. The character, "Ella Cinders," is a reversal of the name "Cinderella" and the wistful and demure Ella proves to be simply Cinderella in modern staging and surroundings. How intrinsically correct this interpretation is we shall see in later discussion.

One of the outstanding traits of the American is his concern for the "underdog," the underprivileged, the hungry, or the needy, which might explain some of the popularity of the story of Cinderella. Perhaps it is because Americans, subconsciously, see in Cinderella something of themselves that this simple folk tale has endeared itself to us for so many years. America is the land of equal opportunity and no man or woman, whatever his station in life, is denied his chance for success and happiness. Indeed, this philosophy goes to the very core of our traditions!

This will only partially explain, however, the continuing drawing power of this classic story of a simple little girl, who longed in her heart to go to the grand festival and meet the Prince. We feel the utmost sympathy for her when she is thwarted in every attempt to attend the dance. Then, finally, by a miracle, she is given a beautiful dress and we thrill with her when the Prince chooses to dance only with her, the poor, forgotten, forlorn little Cinderella! Here is something we all thoroughly enjoy.

Let us for a moment, then, examine the theme in the light of the Scriptures, compare the symbology used therein and discover for ourselves the meanings hidden there for our delight and our illumination.

In reading the passages of the four Gospels, we learn that it was customary for Jesus to teach the people by means of parables. These parables employ the simplest of terms; a child could understand much of what He imparted, so plain were the illustrations He gave of His truth. To make sure that His meaning was understood by His chosen disciples, He later told them the spiritual truths of His stories. Nowhere is the love of Jesus for His twelve friends better shown than in these intimate talks where, point by point, He explained to them the inner meaning of His dissertations before the people.

In reading the stories that come to us out of the old Saxon folklore many have derived great pleasure from them without searching beyond the surface meaning of the tales. But there have been suspicions by a few - and well founded they were - that beneath the surface of the words lay a deeper and more profound essence of meaning. Those who are steeped in the stories contained in the Scriptures, who are well-grounded in the truth that the House of Israel can be traced to the Anglo-Saxon-Celtic peoples on the earth today, will do well to reread this tale, becoming alert to the message that is conveyed to us therein. With an eye to the symbology used, they will discover, not only a similarity, but in many cases an exactitude in the choice of symbols. If they are looking for prophecy in the Bible they will find a corroborative and expanding view out of the deep past into the future in the story of Cinderella.

Today, we have the perspective of two thousand years or more of history to bear out the prophecies of the Bible. As the Israel of God, we have inherited the vast store of Saxon lore, rich in the verification of our ancient origin and overflowing with prophetic assurances concerning our future. Surely God has blessed us with this innate cognizance of our inner worth as His people in direct proportion to our carrying out of His desires and living by His laws.But in the Saxon folk tales He is revealing to all at this time irrefutable evidence that we are His people and that He is to remember us, as a people, in the very near future. World events are shaping up so that we will need the Divine help which He alone can give.

In the story of Cinderella we find more of the teaching of Jesus than in any of the other folk stories, in combination with the covenant relationship of God with His people Israel. It not only identifies Israel as the waiting bride of the Lamb, but describes the preparation she has made, partly under compulsion, for the marriage day which lies ahead.

The ancient seer who created these stories was well versed in the whole Israel tradition, culminating as it does in the life and work of the Master, Jesus. Whether by direct revelation, or by the study of the Scriptures, we do not know; nevertheless, the stories welling up out of Saxony, Denmark and England bespeak a familiarity with all things Biblical. The same secrecy is used, imparting the truth of Israel's identity, using symbols which would be understandable only to Israel herself! In the story of Cinderella, as we shall see, this comprehension comes in reality only by the insight imparted by the Holy Ghost. Through the Holy Ghost all will be revealed at the proper time to the right people in complete harmony with God's great plan for His own.

In the study of the Cinderella tale, then, let us be aware that here is a charming story, wrapped in the gosamer of fairy sheen, which will appeal to the fancy of any youngster. Yet, beneath this array of shining symbols, our author has built upon foundations of basic truth.

To begin with, it is a great racial truth. Around the maiden Cinderella he frames a story of his own people. It is told in terms they will readily understand, just as Jesus taught, using words of the simplest kind, acceptable to the little child. In spinning the tale of Cinderella he has an old, old story to tell, but he had something of prophecy to proclaim as well. And Cinderella has something definite to say to us, different from any of the other Saxon tales.

For the story of Cinderella, the servant girl, is the story of Israel as the race of servers. Israel again takes on the character of a young woman, as she does so often in the Scriptures and in the various folk tales. We hear little of her beauty in this story. To begin with, she is smeared with dirt and dust from the cleaning of the house. Her dress is in rags, covered with ashes, whence comes her name, Cinderella. She has no bed and is so tired from her work at the end of the day that she drops on the hearth before the fireplace and goes to sleep.

Here we are given a hint of her true identity. For what people love the open fire at the hearth better than the Anglo-Saxon-Celtic peoples? The home of the true Anglo-Saxon is "Where the hearth is," and so was it the home of forlorn little Cinderella. She was happiest there. We sense her solace in the fireplace, as so often have others of our race found comfort there.

Jesus, when gathered in the upper room with His disciples, and knowing that He had little time left to be with them on the earth, wished to impart to them the full meaning of His ministry. He also wanted them to know how they should act toward one another and toward the world. He wanted to give them a pattern for behaviour. In the 13th chapter of John we read, "He riseth from supper, and laid aside his garments; and took a towel, and girded himself. After that he poureth water into a basin, and began to wash the disciples'feet, and to wipe them with the towel wherewith he was girded."

After a few moments of amazed silence, Simon Peter protested that the Master should not stoop and wash his feet. And then it was that Jesus sat down at the table and explained to them what He was doing. "Know ye what I have done to you? Ye call me Master and Lord: and ye say well; for so I am. If I then, your Lord and Master, have washed your feet; ye also ought to wash one another's feet. For I have given you an example, that ye should do as I have done to you. Verily, verily I say unto you, the servant is not greater than his Lord; neither he that is sent greater than he that sent him." (John 13:12-16)

This was, in fact, the supreme and final teaching that our Lord left for His disciples, a kind of code for living to be adopted by all true Christians. It suggested that the Christian's life was to be marked by kindness and outward consideration. It also gave him courage to perform distasteful tasks and to face suffering. The condition that

Cinderella found herself in fits this pattern completely.

In the Scriptures Israel is characterized as a servant race, the chosen ones of God, who are to so live that the light of God will shine through them and they, by example, shall lead the rest of mankind into the Christian way of life. "I know whom I have chosen," said Jesus to His disciples on that same fateful night. These disciples are, in type, the twelve tribes of Israel, and to each of them was made a promise which shall be fulfilled upon His return to the earth.

In the story of Cinderella we read, "The two sisters did her every imaginable injury - they mocked her and emptied her peas and lentils into the ashes, so that she was forced to sit and pick them out again. In the evening, when she had worked until she was weary, she had no bed to go to, but had to sleep by the fireside in the ashes. And on that account, they called her Cinderella."

Who are the two sisters and what do they represent? We find a clue when we ask who Israel's tormentors were down through the years of her punishment. Because of her disobedience, God allowed certain forces to have power over the House of Israel for a period of Seven Times (2520 years). The city of Samaria, the capital of the northern ten-tribed Kingdom of Israel, was captured in 721 B. C. by the Assyrians, thus beginning the Great Captivity. This began the time of punishment for the House of Israel, to be followed about a hundred and fifty years later by the capture of Jerusalem and the fall of the House of Judah. It was with the beginning of the reign of Queen Elizabeth I of England that the people of Israel began to emerge from this term of punishment, and also began to carry out their part of God's covenant.

We cannot identify the two sisters without also discovering who their mother was. The answer in the Bible is given in the 17th chapter of Revelation, verse 5. She is: "MYSTERY, BABYLON THE GREAT, THE MOTHER OF HARLOTS AND ABOMINATIONS OF THE EARTH." The mother of the two daughters is the MOTHER OF HARLOTS, and she operates through her two daughters in her two aspects.

The elder one, who asked her stepfather to bring her "beautiful dresses" from the fair, is the ecclesiastical aspect of the Babylonian System, known as "MYSTERY." The younger one, who asked her stepfather to bring her "pearls and jewels," is the other aspect, the economic and commercial manifestation of the Babylonian system, or "BABYLON THE GREAT."

Let us remember that the elder sister, in attempting to trick the Prince into believing that she was the one his heart desired, cut off one of her toes upon the advice of her mother so that she might make her foot small enough to fit the golden shoe. "Cut the toe off: when

28

thou art Queen thou wilt have no more need to go on foot," was the persuasion of the mother. But two white doves gave warning to the Prince, and when he looked down and discovered the bleeding foot, he took the girl back home.

This rebuke of the elder daughter corresponds in history to the rebuke of the power of the Pope in France by Philip the Fair (1303) in an assembly of his nobles, and in England by Henry VIII in the passage of the Act of Supremacy by his parliament, and the launching of the great Reformation movement in Europe. This period was foretold by Jesus to John in the Book of Revelation, when John saw "a mighty angel come down from heaven, clothed with a cloud: and a rainbow was upon his head, and his face was as it were the sun, and his feet as pillars of fire: And he had in his hand a little book open" (Rev. 10:1-2). This Book we know today to be the printed Bible. The printed Word of God, reproduced for the first time as a smaller book, and in quantity, made it possible for all men everywhere to read and study the Bible. The Roman Church, which had sought to deprive mankind of its truth by writing it only in Latin and discouraging the popular reading of the Holy Book, from that time began to lose its power. In England and on the Continent men read the Book and drank deep of the Word of God.

The desire for "beautiful dresses" by the elder daughter links her with this pagan ecclesiastical power, which used brightly-colored and embroidered robes to clothe her priests and the pomp and show of her ceremonies to fasten the attention of the people upon her. With the Reformation these fineries were discarded by those who repudiated the Roman hierarchy; churches were stripped of images and elaborate decorations. Thus, historically speaking, was carried out the rebuke of the elder daughter, upon the discovery of her falsity and her deceit.

The discovery and rejection of the younger daughter has not yet taken place. She is now wearing the golden shoe, with the blood gushing from her foot. For the younger daughter is the Babylonian System of modern economics, and business today has its foundations set in greedy struggle, in destructive competition, in war. The blood streaming from her foot is the blood of countless men, women and children who have died through the heartless atrocities of war.

The destruction of this abominable system is foretold in the 18th chapter of Revelation and is yet future. A pleading voice is heard by John, saying, "Come out of her, my people, that ye be not partakers of her sins, and that ye receive not of her plagues." (Rev. 18:4) Can this voice, calling to us, be the voice of the Holy Ghost? For it was the song of two white pigeons that warned the Prince that the two daughters were trying to deceive him.

How quickly, then, will the Prince of Peace recognize the deceit of this younger one when He comes, and rebuke this system parading in

His name and seeking admittance into His Kingdom. By the power of Holy Ghost, Jesus Christ is given to see, and to act upon, the falsity of this presumption of Mammon, and the second usurper is refused admittance to His Kingdom and His Throne. Jesus, in his earthly ministry, rebuked this same system of Mammon (Luke 16:11-13), saying that no man can serve both God and Mammon. How much more powerfully will He cast it away, condemning it to destruction, when He comes again to be our reigning King!

The two stepsisters having asked their new father for finery and jewels, Cinderella, in direct contrast, mustered the courage to ask her father to bring her "the first branch of a tree that knocks against your hat on the way home." Cinderella's desire for only "a branch of a tree" in lieu of all the fine things her father might have brought her from the fair is a remarkable identification mark, for there is a deep spiritual meaning in this strange request. We see Cinderella's character portrayed by her choice of the simple, natural things, in preference to material, man-made things. But beyond this the symbology of the "branch of a tree" is very closely related to the Scriptures. Here we get a glimpse of Israel in her role of royalty.

In chapter 17 of Ezekiel we read of a riddle which was a special message from God, through Ezekiel, to the House of Israel. How does this riddle apply to our story? There are two eagles in the riddle and the first eagle, "a great eagle with great wings," refers to the establishment of the Zarah branch of the tribe of Judah in Ireland when it is said, "He took the highest branch of the cedar: he cropped off the top of his young twigs, and carried it into a land of traffick; he set it in a city of merchants" (Ez. 17:3-4). The Zarah branch had migrated years ahead of Jeremiah to Ireland and it was a son of the Zarah line, who was to welcome the daughter of Zedekiah, to the new land "by great waters." (Atlantic Ocean)

The cedar of Lebanon is symbolic of royalty, and within this riddle is concealed the series of happenings that became history - the continuation of the royal line with the marriage of the daughter of Zedekiah to a prince of the scarlet thread, i.e., of the Zarah branch of Judah, a king in his own right.

We now see a close analogy here with the "plucking of the branch" by the father of Cinderella, who brought it home to her. "Cinderella thanked him, and went to her mother's grave and planted the branch on it, and wept so much that the tears fell down on it and watered it. It grew, however, and became a handsome tree." The use of the symbol of a "branch of a tree," therefore, has a connotation of royalty, for Cinderella is herself emblematic of the "tender twig" transported by the great eagle from Palestine to the "isles" of the west,"planted in a fruitful field" where "it grew,and became a spreading vine."

This is borne out in the story by the fact that when Cinderella went to the ball she was chosen by the prince for the dance, to the exclusion of all others. Indeed, the similarity in experience is very plain in that the identity of the Throne of David is well concealed even to this day, just as the identity of the princess (Cinderella) was not known until the prince himself had searched her out. As the day approaches when our Lord will return and claim His throne and His "princess," it will be more and more evident to all that the House of David has continued without a break from the time of King David to this very day.

The comforting presence of the Holy Ghost is distinctly brought out in the story of Cinderella. Having received the branch, she planted it and, watered with her tears, it grew into a tree. On a branch of the tree a white bird came to sit "and if Cinderella expressed a wish the bird threw down to her what she had wished for." This bird was a very conspicuous agent of blessing to Cinderella, at times when all the world seemed turned against her.

It is easily recognized as the symbol used in the Bible to announce the visitation of the Holy Ghost. For this bird is a dove, denoting the influx of the Holy Ghost, so beautifully described at the baptism of Jesus in the River Jordan: "And Jesus, when he was baptized, went up straightway out of the water: and, lo, the heavens were opened unto him, and he saw the Spirit of God descending like a dove" (Matt. 3:16). Luke also describes the event: "And the Holy Ghost descended in a bodily shape like a dove upon him. " (Luke 3:22)

The dove (or the Holy Ghost) came to Cinderella in her moments of loneliness and desolation when she was seated under her tree, meditating upon her sorry condition. So shall those of Israel receive the gift of the Holy Ghost when they are most needful of God's help, as promised by Jesus upon his departure from the earth: "Ye shall receive power, after that the Holy Ghost is come upon you: and ye shall be witnesses unto me both in Jerusalem, and in all Judaea, and in Samaria, and unto the uttermost part of the earth" (Acts 1:8). Jesus clearly foresaw the need for some sustaining power to hold the Christians steadfast in the faith, and his parting gift to his followers was the comfort and guidance of the Holy Ghost.

With this spiritual power acting through the overcomers, His Gospel spread throughout the world. The Bible, when translated into English, went with the English-speaking peoples wherever they settled upon the globe. They formed missionary societies, finally fulfilling to the letter the command of the Master, "Go ye into all the world, and preach the gospel to every creature." With the expansion of the British Empire, and the forming of the United States of America, the sons of Isaac were intent upon their mission of spreading the Gospel everywhere they went, even to the farthest corners of the earth.

The reference to the ashes that clung to Cinderella's dress alludes to a period of mourning, of course, and refers to the sorrowful endurance of the "times" of punishment visited by God upon the House of Israel. She knows that she has broken God's laws and must pay the penalty in her own life. This period is referred to in the 11th chapter of Revelation, verse 3: "And I will give power unto my two witnesses, and they shall prophesy a thousand two hundred and three-score days [years], clothed in sackcloth." Ashes and sackcloth are always associated with a time of mourning and refer to the time when Cinderella sat alone and, in sadness of heart, endured the mocking and avarice of her two stepsisters. Except for the visits of the doves (the Holy Ghost as the Comforter), she might have lost heart under the onslaught of their ridicule and torment. She is clearly identified here with the "two witnesses," which are "the two olive trees, and the two candlesticks standing before the God of the earth." (Rev. 11:4)

We are all familiar with that part of our story which tells of the invitations given to the two elder sisters to attend the King's festival and dance, and of the yearning of Cinderella that she might go also. Yet she is frustrated by her stepmother and sisters in her efforts for lack of a proper gown. The meanness of her new relatives is nowhere more clearly illustrated than in this passage, where they taunt her, "Thou go, Cinderella! Thou art dusty and dirty, and wouldst go to the festival? Thou hast no clothes and shoes, and yet wouldst dance!"

Then she was forced to continue on with her customary chore of picking her lentils out of the ashes, in the hopes that she might do so "in two hours" and thus be able to have a dress and shoes and go to the ball with her sisters. Let us remember that it was not her mother or her sisters who finally give her the dress and the golden shoes (which fit no one but Cinderella); it was the dove who granted her heart's desire: "Then the bird threw a gold and silver dress down to her, and slippers embroidered with silk and silver. She put on the dress with all speed, and went to the festival. Her stepmother, how-ever, did not know her. . . ."

This passage bespeaks the rescuing power of the Holy Ghost, which, when a Christian calls forth that power and uses it, draws him close to God and places him in a position to receive an invitation to the great festival of our Lord. And we shall be properly attired for that magnificent event; we may be sure of that.

The beautiful dress and slippers given to Cinderella by the white bird suggest the "wedding garments" of Revelation: "And to her was granted that she should be arrayed in fine linen, clean and white: for the fine linen is the righteousness of saints." (Rev. 19:8) It is indi-cated here that none may wear these garments but those who are spiritually prepared to receive them. It is not the garments them-selves that we shall wish for, but when we are cleansed within and have made way for the indwelling Christ, we shall automatically receive from God the necessary apparel for the great and wonderful Marriage Supper of our Lord.

And, as our story indicates, it is through humble and obedient service, as so often demonstrated by Jesus, that the overcomer can earn these vestments and so be ready to enter into the restored Kingdom of Heaven to be established upon the earth. Cinderella, the quiet and contemplative server, through the intercession of the white dove (the Holy Ghost), prepared herself for the coming of her Prince. "Blessed are they which are called unto the marriage supper of the Lamb" are the words of Jesus himself, given through his beloved disciple, John, in Revelation 19:9.

"The King appointed the festival" and any or all may identify themselves with Cinderella and come to the festival, for Cinderella in her new dress represents the cleansed Israel of God. All are invited who desire to attend, but unless we wear the clean linen of righteousness, we may not be found acceptable when the festival begins.

There is a remarkable similarity between the festival of our story and the parable of the King's marriage feast described by Matthew, chapter 22:2-14; particularly the care with which the King watched what his guests wore: "And when the king came in to see the guests, he saw there a man which had not on a wedding garment: And he said unto him, Friend, how camest thou in hither not having a wedding garment? And he was speechless. Then the king said to the servants: Bind him hand and foot, and take him away. . . ." Thus we see that the conditions for entry into the wedding feast are definite and certain and the Lord will know who has properly attired himself for the celebration of the feast.

In our story the Prince will dance with only one person, his Princess, at the ball. He has no eye for any other. She is recognized by him for what she truly is.

It is evident in our story that the festival represents the time of the First Resurrection, when the Prince comes and takes those to Himself who have prepared themselves through service performed in His name. Israel (Cinderella) is the bride, but before the marriage comes the Marriage Supper, at which time the Bridegroom joins with His friends in the festival of rejoicing. The true marriage ceremony comes later, and is the culmination of the banquet that precedes it.

This festival is a kind of induction into office of those who are to rule with Him, but the Prince has not yet come to begin His rule. He has invited to the feast those whom He wants to assist Him in His future rulership, and these represent the true Church, the members of the body of Christ. These are the ones who are to be rewarded for their faithfulness and their steadfastness in the kingdom rule ahead.

The time of the rulership of the Prince is described in Revelation 21:1-2 in John's words of awe: "I saw a new heaven and a new earth: for the first heaven and the first earth were passed away. . . . And I, John, saw the holy city, new Jerusalem, coming down from God out of heaven, prepared as a bride adorned for her husband. And I heard a great voice out of heaven saying, Behold, the tabernacle of God is with men, and he will dwell with them, and they shall be his people, and God himself shall be with them, and be their God."

This time of rulership is only inferred in the story of Cinderella, for the story ends with the marriage of the Prince and his Princess. But he is happy with his bride, who was identified for him by the song of two white doves singing to him from the branch of a hazel tree:

> "Turn and peep, turn and peep,
> No blood is in the shoe,
> The shoe is not too small for her,
> The true bride rides with you."

HANSEL AND GRETHEL

Few of the fairy tales have quite the Germanic flavor that we find in the story of Hansel and Grethel. Perhaps it is the forest background for the plot which links it in our minds with the forested parts of northern Europe. Certainly, the little gingerbread house has its associations in our minds as we read of the two children coming into a clearing and finding the house all covered with cakes and candy. Saxon children have dreamed of such dainties for centuries and Saxon parents have rewarded their children with sugared gingerbread down through the years. It is traditional in Germany and in Holland even to this day: "pfeffer-kuchen" (gingerbread) is a delicacy which every child looks forward to, especially at holiday times.

There is no story, therefore, that has quite the appeal to children as the story of Hansel and Grethel because of its associations with candy and cakes. And the story is probably as familiar to us as any ever told. Our hearts are touched when we read of the lack of food in the household of the little family of four; our sympathy goes out to the two children when we read of the plan of the mother to lose them deep in the forest, with only a crust of bread and a little fire to keep them warm. We feel sorry for the father as this scheme is presented to him, and for the children, who overhear the plan for their disposal in the forest.

Later we feel the anguish of spirit that visited these two as they plodded wearily through the forest and experienced the most extreme feeling of loneliness imaginable. Hungry, unwanted, without direction, we follow them to where they found the little clearing in the woods. There before them, to their astonishment, sat the little gingerbread house, all decorated with cake and candy. What a delight to their joyful eyes! What a picture of ecstasy: Hansel running to break off a piece of the cake roof and calling to Grethel to help herself to some of the sugar candy pane! This is a picture as captivating to us as the memories we have of our own childhood. What is more natural than that they should assuage their hunger with these pretty things to eat?

Little did they realize that a witch had built this house as a trap; nor did they know that they would be held prisoner within its walls. They were to learn, in time, that the vindictive scheme was that they themselves were to be eaten in return for these bits of sweets, by which they were being baited.

Our discovery of the symbolism hidden within the structure of the story of Hansel and Grethel permits us to approach the story of the children of Israel with new enlightenment. For this story is but another of the many Saxon folk tales which give us the details of the wanderings of the children of Israel after they left the captivity of the

Assyrians, during a period of which we have scant historical record.

It is for this reason that these fairy tales are of such value to the modern reader of the Bible, who seeks a true understanding of his heritage and a full comprehension of the story the Bible tells. Reading these stories he begins to realize that they connect him with the ten lost tribes of Israel taken captive by Tiglath-Pileser III in 721 B C. And in reading the present story he finds that it also deals with the House of Judah, taken captive to Babylon by King Nebuchadnezzar some time later. The reader will discover how the author has reached far back into Israel tradition, to the days of Jacob, when he joined his twelve sons in their sojourn in Egypt. Certain symbols used are familiar to us; others are completely new. The latter are born of the new environment in which the children of Israel found themselves; they fit the new character of the people.

It is with this set of new symbols that we may make a fresh approach to the Bible. While many of the actual happenings of history are here wrapped in the garments of so-called fairy tale lore, we can, if we will, discern the truth lying beneath their outer covering. We discover, also, that God had a reason for permitting this to be so, for in His great plan for his people He has hidden from them for a time their own identity. Yet this identity is carefully concealed in the symbology of the books of the Bible (particularly in the Book of Revelation).

Not many Christians today realize the significance of the fact that, after the reign of Solomon, Israel was divided into two kingdoms: the northern ten-tribed kingdom, thereafter known as the House of Israel, with its capital at Samaria in the north, and the House of Judah, which remained at Jerusalem. The whole import of this division into two kingdoms cannot be fully comprehended except in terms of the historical happenings extending from that day to this--particularly the fact that the modern representatives of the House of Israel are the Anglo-Saxon-Celtic peoples. The interlinked destiny of the House of Israel and the House of Judah is carefully recognized in the story of Hansel and Grethel.

In this story we have a specific reference to the House of Judah. Here the author has joined the two houses together as brother and sister; he has put them hand in hand, one comforting and calming the fears of the other as they wander through the darkness of the forest. Theirs was a mother who was interested primarily in herself and her own self-preservation, while it was their father whose heart was wrung with anguish that he must be separated from his children. If Hansel is Judah and Grethel is Israel, who, in our story, is their father and mother?

The mother of Hansel and Grethel lacked the selfless affection which characterizes a true mother. She was more like a stepmother, such as the stepmother of Cinderella. In relation to Israel she is here representative of that part of Babylon worship which emerged in Palestine and in Egypt as the worship of Baal, which, in the Book of Revelation, is referred to as "MYSTERY, BABYLON." It is with a strange kind of poetic license that the spinner of this tale creates a mother for Hansel and Grethel who is both greedy and self-centered, so much so that she will sacrifice her children to her own preservation by turning them out to die in the wilderness. This characterization of an unnatural mother will best be understood as we proceed with our study of the story and relate it to other happenings as recorded in the Old Testament of the Bible.

The identity of the father in our story is disclosed by his condition of near-starvation. His children representing the twelve tribes of Israel there is only one man in the Bible who answers this description: Jacob! To be sure, Joseph was sold into slavery and rose to a place of great power in Egypt. But it was during a time of famine in Canaan that Jacob sent his sons into Egypt to buy corn, and we will see how this relates to our story.

In the Bible the account is given of only two times of exodus of the people of Israel out of the land of Canaan, the land that was given to them by God. The first exodus was by the progenitors of the twelve tribes themselves, the sons of Jacob. The first exodus was because of lack of food in the land of Canaan and in the home of Jacob; hence its association with our story. The opening words of the fairy tale state:

"Hard by a great forest dwelt a poor woodcutter [Jacob] with his wife and his two children. . . He had little to bite and to break, and once, when great scarcity fell on the land, he could no longer provide daily bread."

A corresponding condition will be found in the Bible in Genesis 41:56-57 and 42:1-3. It is a condition fitting exactly that of our wood-chopper, who sent his two children (symbolic of the twelve children of Jacob) out to forage for food. In the Bible account it was Jacob who sacrificed his high affection for his sons (even to Benjamin, his favorite) when he sent them down to Egypt for corn.

"And the famine was over all the face of the earth: and Joseph opened all the storehouses, and sold unto the Egyptians; and the famine waxed sore in the land of Egypt. And all countries came into Egypt to Joseph to buy corn; because that the famine was so sore in all lands. Now when Jacob saw that there was corn in Egypt, Jacob said unto his sons, Why do ye look one upon another? And he said, Behold, I have heard that there is corn in Egypt: get you down thither, and buy for us from thence; that we may live, and not die. And Joseph's ten brethren went down to buy corn in Egypt." (Gen. 41:56-57; 42:1-3)

As a result of this journey to Egypt and the disclosure that Joseph was their brother, the eleven brothers were persuaded by Joseph to go down and live in Egypt.

"Haste ye, and go up to my father, and say unto him, Thus saith thy son Joseph, God hath made me lord of all Egypt: come down unto me, tarry not: and thou shalt dwell in the land of Goshen." (Gen. 45: 9-10.)

It is important at this point to remember that with Jacob and his sons went the stone of Bethel. This was the stone upon which Jacob had laid his head when he dreamed of "angels of God ascending and descending." (Gen. 28:12) When he woke he made a vow:

"If God will be with me, and will keep me in this way that I go, and will give me bread to eat, and raiment to put on, so that I come again unto my father's house in peace; then shall the Lord be my God: and this stone, which I have set for a pillar, shall be God's house." (Gen. 28:20-22.)

This was the stone that Jacob and his sons carried with them wherever they went, as it was a symbol to them of their covenant with God. It was by the grace of this covenant, and under the leadership of Moses, that the children of Israel were to be delivered out of Egypt and "find their way back home." Here we have a direct connection in the two stories with the use of the symbol of "the stone." In the Bible story the word is used in the singular, while in the folk story it is employed in the plural.

To turn to the story, when Hansel overheard his father and mother discussing their lack of food and their plan to place the children in the forest to forage for themselves, he went outside and put into his pocket some small stones. Using these stones he planned to "find his way back home" through the wilderness, dropping the stones in the path as they made their way along. The "stones" are here identified with the "stone of Bethel," carried by the sons of Jacob into Egypt. For the stone accompanied the twelve sons of Jacob on their journey to Egypt and also returned with their descendants, the twelve tribes of Israel, to Canaan under the leadership of Moses. In the story it was the means by which Hansel and Grethel (the twelve tribes) found their way back home (Canaan) after being lost in the wilderness (Egypt).

When Hansel overheard his parents planning a second time to abandon him and his sister in the forest, he sought to go out again and gather some pebble-stones in order that he might mark his way back home. But this time he found the door had been locked, so that he could not get out to gather the stones. Nevertheless, he comforted his little sister, reassuring her with the words, "Do not cry, Grethel, go to sleep quietly, the good God will help us."

The next day Hansel took the bread that was given them to eat, broke it into small pieces, and scattered it along the way as they were again led into the forest. He hoped, by aid of the moonlight, to find his way back home by these pieces of bread, just as he had by following the pebble-stones. But his plans were upset. "When the moon came out, they set out, but they found no crumbs, for the many thousands of birds which fly about in the woods and fields had picked them all up."

Here we see the compulsory action of the laws of God, forbidding the children of Israel to return to their homeland. This applied to the House of Judah as well as the House of Israel, for the second exodus of the children of Israel from their homeland was into Assyria and Babylon, this time by force of arms. To be sure, the House of Israel was taken about a hundred and thirty years before Judah, but both paid the same penalty for their disregard of God's laws.

"For so it was that the children of Israel had sinned against the Lord their God . . . and walked in the statutes of the heathen . . . and they left all the commandments of the Lord their God. . . . Therefore the Lord was very angry with Israel, and removed them out of his sight: there was none left but the tribe of Judah only. Also Judah kept not the commandments of the Lord their God, but walked in the statutes of Israel which they made." (II Kings 17:7-19.)

Judah also was punished by deportation and found herself taken captive to Babylon, even as Israel had been taken into Assyria many years before.

Because they are all of the same origin (though separated into two groups), our Saxon scribe has represented Israel and Judah as being taken away together from their homeland in the Great Captivities. But it is highly significant that the stone of Bethel did not go with them. This stone, the token of God's covenant, was temporarily taken from them. Abandoned in the temple at Jerusalem, it became the Divinely-assigned task of Jeremiah to take it, together with the daughters of Zedekiah, the Ark of the Covenant and other relics, to Egypt and thence by sea to northern Ireland. The "seven times" of punishment (2520 years) had begun for the children of Israel and all that might connect them with their past was severed. Except for a very small portion of Judah who returned to Jerusalem, and a part of Benjamin and Levi, the children of Israel were truly "lost in the forest" and also lost to history.

The House of Judah, then, followed the House of Israel out of northern Persia across southern Russia and central Europe to Normandy, Denmark and Germany (Jutland: land of the Jutes or Judahites). Indeed, a part of the Zarah branch of the House of Judah had already gone on to what is now Scotland and England by sea and land at the time of their first enslavement in Egypt. They were to be joined by the House of Israel later, and most of the remainder of the Pharez branch of the House of Judah, in this faraway land. The latter came, determined to lead a new life, to find a land where they would be free to follow the commandments of God. This land was the same described by Isaiah as the "Isles" of the west, meaning Ireland, Scotland, England and Wales (Isaiah 49:1 and 60:9), and subsequently the Americas, Australia and New Zealand.

In Esdras 13:42 it is said of the children of Israel that, after their succumbing to the worship of the Mother of Heaven in Egypt and of Baal in the land of Canaan, and their subsequent punishment of captivity in Persia, there arose in them a desire "to leave the heathen population, and go to a more distant region, where the human race had never lived, so that there perhaps they might keep their statutes, which they had not kept in their own country." Just as Israel had resolved on a new life, in a new land, where she could be free to live according to God's laws, so, too, there were many of Judah who decided upon the same course.

The "pieces of bread" which Hansel scattered, and which were devoured by the birds, are of interest as an example of the use of symbology in these Saxon folk tales. In John 6:35 Jesus said, "I am the bread of life: he that cometh to me shall never hunger. . . ." Bread represents the inspired "word of God" to the overcomers, the truth, and is intimately associated with the Holy Spirit of God. Again, in relation to the activities of the Holy Spirit, we meet up with "birds" who pick up the bread along the way. And again it is a white bird who leads the lost children through the woods to the place where they find the little house. The white bird, as in the story of Cinderella, represents the descent of the "Holy Spirit." In this case it represents the "leading of the way" by the Holy Spirit of God. It was by this means, and this alone, that the children of Israel were led and protected as they proceeded on their way to the shores of the British Isles.

In the same way, it may be said, the Holy Spirit of God has done its perfect work in preserving the truth of the Anglo-Saxon heritage through the creation of the Saxon folk tales. Actually, these tales are records of the flight of these people and they are dropped, like pieces of bread, along the way so that the children of Israel may discover the truth of their own origin. By the grace and gift of the Holy Spirit these "bread crumbs" become exceedingly meaningful to their readers. It is to be hoped that God's people will partake of them anew, with the insight which comes only of the Holy Spirit, so that their true meaning may now be revealed. It is part of the marvel of God's ways that He reveals all things to all men in time. But certain truths He veils in mystery until the proper hour.

We will also note that, having been led to the cottage by the little white bird, the cottage itself is described as "built of bread and covered with cakes." The cottage signifies England, as we have already discovered in our study of the story of Snow-white. But here we have a cottage built of bread. This clearly describes the early faith of the English Church, founded as early as 38 A D by Joseph of Arimathea and his followers. It describes a church born of the simple words and admonitions of Jesus; a Christian church that grew and expanded in this fertile soil, unspoiled by the pagan practices so rampant in the countries around the Mediterranean Sea.

But we will also notice that this bread is "covered with cakes." What is the significance here? The determination of the children of Israel to return to the laws of God and so to rededicate their lives according to the words of Jesus was glossed over with the "fancy icing and sugar" of the pagan ritual that followed them to the place where they had fled.

The cake with which the bread of the cottage was covered bespeaks the pomp and show of pagan religious worship; it is that which is designed to attract the eye, with little intent to satisfy the soul. Hansel and Grethel found little of nourishment in this kind of fare. The word "gingerbread" has come to have a colloquial meaning to us stemming possibly from this very story. When someone says a thing is "all gingerbread," we know exactly what is meant.

In this case the cake, or gingerbread, designates that long-armed invasion of England by the Roman Church in the year 657 A D, when Pope Vitalian raised up an Archbishop for the first time and ordered the services to be said in Latin. The people of England were beguiled into this type of worship and accepted the use of painted images in their churches, the burning of incense and the colorful embroidered robes with which the priests bedecked themselves. The pomp began to equal that of Rome itself and England was ensnared.

Equally so a snare was set for Hansel and Grethel and we read that, as the children began to nibble on the cake and candy, they heard a soft voice that spoke from within:

Nibble, nibble, gnaw,
Who is nibbling at my little house?"
"Suddenly the door opened, and a very, very old woman, who supported herself on crutches, came creeping out. Hansel and Grethel were so terribly frightened that they let fall what they had in their hands. The old woman, however, nodded her head and said, 'Oh you dear children, Who has brought you here? Do come in and stay with me. No harm shall happen to you.'"

We at once recognize the old woman in this story, for she is the very same old woman who came to see Snow-white, peddling her pretty wares. In this instance she herself lives in the little cottage, and it is the fancy covering that she puts on the house that attracts the children. Here again she represents the irresistible power of the

Church of Rome which, while it offered the people of Israel a front of friendliness and a show of finery and cakes, actually had quite a different design and purpose. History reveals the abuses suffered by England at the hands of Rome, and how finally this hold upon her was broken and thrown off, once and for all.

So the old woman put on an act of friendliness:

"Good food was set before them; milk and pancakes, with sugar, apples and nuts. Afterwards two pretty little beds were covered with clean white linen, and Hansel and Grethel lay down in them, and thought they were in heaven."

We know, however, that this was only pretense:

"She was in reality a wicked witch, who lay in wait for the children, and had only built the little house in order to entice them there. When a child fell into her power, she killed it, cooked and ate it, and that was a feast day with her."

We can recognize this same woman by turning in the Scriptures to the 17th chapter of Revelation where she is described as "arrayed in purple and scarlet colour, and decked with gold and precious stones and pearls [the children found these things in the witch's room when they fled from the cottage]. . . . And I saw the woman drunken with the blood of the saints, and with the blood of the martyrs of Jesus: and when I saw her, I wondered with great admiration."

This creature naturally drew the attention of John as he gazed upon her and he found it worth-while to mention that she seemed to cast a spell over all who beheld her. What better description can be given of the fate of the true believers in Jesus at the hands of the Roman Church, which instituted the great Inquisition, torturing and taking the lives of countless helpless believers. The Inquisition was felt worse in Spain and France, but its terror spread throughout the whole of Europe. This woman is definitely identified with Rome, the city, and all the evil that emanated from it: "The seven heads are seven mountains, on which the woman sitteth." (Rev. 17:9) Rome is famed as the "City of the Seven Hills" upon which the city is spread.

At one with this theme of Revelation is the theme of our story. Well fed upon her food, poor Hansel began to realize he was being fattened up to be eaten. Then the witch "seized him with her shriveled hand, carried him into the little stable, and shut him in with a grated door." We are familiar with that part of the story where Grethel was made to work and cook, then was fed nothing herself but crab shells. We also are familiar with the ruse used by Hansel to ward off his fate by putting forth a bone for the old woman to feel when she came around to test him to decide if he was plump enough to eat.

This episode reflects the awakening of the Englishman to the real intent of the Roman Church, which was gaining a temporal power in a realm to which she had no title. King Henry VIII appears to have expressed the wishes of the people better than he knew when he broke with the Pope. The English Parliament only too readily passed the Act of Reformation and the Act of Supremacy, returning to the English sovereign the right to appoint his own bishops. As the anointed ruler and inheritor of the Throne of David, he was reinstated as the spiritual head of the Church of England. Except for the short reign of Mary Tudor, the ruler of England has retained this power, and this obligation, to the people.

We read with joy of the quick demise of the witch when Grethel, by a clever trick, pushed the witch into the oven and she was burned to death. This passage parallels in the Scriptures the 2nd verse of Revelation 18 when John "saw another angel come down from heaven, having great power; and the earth was lightened with his glory. And he cried mightily with a strong voice, saying, Babylon the great is fallen, is fallen!" Thus the ecclesiastical aspect of the power of Babylon (Mystery) is here shown as having begun its decline. This decline was reflected in history chiefly by the great Reformation movement, a spark which was fanned to flames in nearly every country of Europe, as well as England.

The burning of the witch in the story would seem to include also the collapse of the economic structure built upon Babylon, which still holds sway in the world today:

"Therefore shall her plagues come in one day, death, and mourning, and famine; and she shall be utterly burned with fire: for strong is the Lord God who judgeth her." (Rev. 18:8.)

Assuming that the witch represents Babylon in all its varied phases, we must conclude that our story passes at this point from history into prophecy. By the very nature of the next phase of the story, this is evident.

The two children flee from the place where they have been held captive and start out in search of home. "When they had walked for two hours, they came to a great piece of water. 'We cannot get over,' said Hansel, 'I see no footplank, and no bridge.' 'And no boat crosses either,' answered Grethel, 'but a little white duck is swimming there; if I ask her, she will help us over.'" Then she cried:

"Little duck, little duck, dost thou see,
Hansel and Grethel are waiting for thee?
There's never a plank, or bridge in sight,
Take us across on thy back so white."

Now, what is the symbolical meaning of the "great piece of water?" The children had not encountered this body of water in going from their home to the place in the forest where they found the cake-covered cottage. Why, on their return, should they find this barrier to their path, over which there was no bridge, and for which they had no boat in order to cross?

It is indeed significant that Grethel (Israel) spied a white duck gliding on the water, to which she called for help to get across. Again we meet up with a familiar symbol, the symbol of the Holy Spirit, this time a white bird in the form of a duck. The duck, of course, is quite at home on the water, and herein lies a clue to an explanation of this "piece of water" lying in their way. This passage portrays in very vivid terms the events of the first resurrection, which is briefly described in the 12th verse of the 11th chapter of Revelation:

"And they heard a great voice from heaven saying unto them, Come up hither. And they ascended up to heaven in a cloud."

The body of water which they must cross is symbolic of the ascension out of that which is material into that which is Divine. There is no material aid available in the crossing of this water. There is no obvious way to cross, and to most, it is illogical to assume that it can be done at all. But Grethel (Israel), by the simple faith that lay in her heart, looked to the white duck (the Holy Spirit) and knew that in this way she and Hansel could get across and arrive home safe. Home, of course, is the Kingdom of Heaven.

In the beginning, the home that was given to the children of Israel was the land of Canaan. When God established there His kingdom with the crowning of David, he gave them a capital city in their land, which we know as Jerusalem. It was only by the disobedience of His children that God allowed the Kingdom to be destroyed (to all outward appearances) and the people were sent into strange lands. Herein lies the hidden drama of the story of Hansel and Grethel, that, after their wandering as "lost" in the forest, they met up with the witch in the cottage in the forest, and after near death in the trap set for them by the witch, they escaped and tried to find their way back home.

But the home to which they returned was not the home they had left. It lay beyond a large piece of water. And when they were transported to this home by the paddling of the duck (the power of the Holy Spirit), they found that it was a different home, and far happier than the one they left. The old woman (the false mother in the story) was dead. She was denied entry into this new home. But they did find their father (God) and rushed into his arms.

We have a good description of this "heavenly home" by turning to John's experience (Rev. 20:4) when he stood and "saw thrones, and they sat upon them, and judgment was given unto them: and I saw the souls of them that were beheaded for the witness of Jesus, and for the word of God, and which had not worshipped the beast, neither his image, neither had received his mark upon their foreheads, or in their hands; and they lived and reigned with Christ a thousand years."

In the same passage of Revelation we read:

"Blessed and holy is he that hath part in the first resurrection: on such the second hath no power, but they shall be priests of God and of Christ, and shall reign with him a thousand years." (Rev. 20:6.)

The return of Hansel and Grethel to their home also includes the joy of "a new heaven and a new earth: for the first heaven and the first earth were passed away; and there was no more sea" (Rev. 21:1). They have become a part of the "new Jerusalem, coming down from God out of heaven, prepared as a bride adorned for her husband" (Rev. 21:2). Truly, it may be said of these joyous children that God, their father, "shall wipe away all tears from their eyes; and [for them] there shall be no more death, neither sorrow, nor crying, neither shall there be any more pain: for the former things are passed away." (Rev. 21:4)

The parabolical story of Hansel and Grethel is another of the Anglo-Saxon tales that tells the story of the misdeeds of the children of Israel and their subsequent punishment for those misdeeds. It supplies evidence of the fact that a large portion of the House of Judah followed the House of Israel northward and westward out of Persia. Joining with Israel, they went through the Great Purge with them, from which they shall emerge ready to accept the new responsibility of Kingdom administration. At that time the prophecy of the 37th chapter of Ezekiel will be fulfilled, according to the promise God made to him:

"And I will make them one nation in the land upon the mountains of Israel; and one king shall be king to them all: and they shall be no more two nations, neither shall they be divided into two kingdoms any more at all. . . . And David my servant shall be king over them; and they all shall have one shepherd: they shall also walk in my judgments, and observe my statutes, and do them. . . . Moreover, I will make a covenant of peace with them; it shall be an everlasting covenant with them: and I will place them, and multiply them, and will set my sanctuary in the midst of them forevermore. My tabernacle also shall be with them: yea, I will be their God, and they shall be my people." (Ez. 37:22, 24, 26-27.)

The story of Hansel and Grethel bears witness to the truth of the re-establishment of the "good figs" of Judah (Jer. 24), together with the House of Israel and the tribe of Benjamin, in a new covenant with God, which shall never be broken. The signal for the evolvement of this new order will be the manifestation of the phenomena of the First Resurrection. Thus we may conclude that this early Saxon story is a part of our heritage of prophecy. Understanding the symbology used in its composition, we can also accept it as a part of the records of our racial past, linking us directly with Abraham, Isaac and Jacob and their descendants, the Israel of God - the people whom God blessed so long ago with his covenant, and to whom He made great promises. For those who are able to discern the "signs of the times" it should be evident that the time for the fulfillment of these promises is at hand and each should be joyous and alert in anticipation of the great events which lie directly ahead.

**English village of
Ringmore, near
Plymouth**

JACK AND THE BEANSTALK

"Fee, Fi Fo Fum! I smell the blood of an Englishman!" These words are known by many a school boy who, on more than one occasion, has used this magic incantation to punctuate his play. They are words as famous as any in the English language and, when they are heard, the great giant in the story of Jack and the Beanstalk springs to life and can be heard tromping into his house with three calves strung by the heels from his belt. One can immediately picture poor Jack quivering in the oven where he had been hidden by the tall woman of the giant's house. All of the details of this captivating story return to one's mind as vividly as when the story was first heard in childhood.

Here is a story that has penetrated the very fibre of the English language and traditions. Its popularity even to this day bespeaks its basic appeal and betrays the intrinsic genius of its creator. Yes, the story of Jack, the giant-killer, ranks high among the fairy stories, emerging from a rich Anglo-Saxon past to take its place with them as a record, however imaginative, of the evolvement of that race from small beginnings to a great responsibility and destiny by a process of gradual, spiritual growth. Here, in this familiar story, we find another of the many keys that unlock the mystery of the disappearance of the ten tribes of Israel from the records of history.

It is the clever device of a master mind that clothes a great truth within the intricacies of a parable, or a story. The saga of a great people, and a great race, has been carefully wrapped within the folds of a children's tale. What better method could have been chosen by this sage of long ago than to perpetuate vital historical facts within the eager and imaginative mind of a child, so recently a part of the mind of God? What more formative material could be used in preserving this great racial truth than that which we find in the Saxon fairy tales? For each, in its own way, holds a vital part of this truth, which, when pieced together, paint a magnificent and somewhat overwhelming picture equalled in majesty only by the final passages of the Book of Revelation?

As we shall discover, many of the meanings in the story of Jack and the Beanstalk are corroborated by this and other books of the Bible. Its symbolism understood, the story becomes a classic among Anglo-Israel chronicles and is another link to restore the chain of events that lead us back directly to the time of Abraham in the Bible. Much revered as the story may be in the hearts of all who have heard it, especially children, as a record of the Anglo-Saxon-Celtic race it takes on a new and doubled significance. So let us turn to the story itself.

There are six characters in this drama. If we comprehend what these characters stand for as symbols, we will get the meaning of the story. Three of these characters are man and three are women. In the first category is Jack, then the "man with the enchanted beans," and finally the giant, or ogre, as he is sometimes called. The women are, first, the mother of Jack, then the old woman he met on his way to the giant's house and, finally, the "great, tall woman standing in the doorway of the stately mansion." We will study each of these characters in turn and, when we find out who they are, we shall arrive at some very vital conclusions. With these conclusions we shall know more of the missing links of Anglo-Israel history and by this see that the author of the tale was a prophet. He was a prophet as truly as any of those found in the Bible, for his prophecies coincide closely with those of the Scriptures and also elaborate upon them.

Let us look first at Jack, for if we can understand who he is, we shall have largely solved the enigma of the story. He is the central figure and the hero of the tale. Indeed, what happens to him is the whole theme of it, and therefore of chief interest to us. In the name "Jack" we find a shortened form of the name "Jacob." Jack, therefore stands for the same Jacob of the Bible who had twelve fine sons and who, because God found him worthy, was given the spiritual name of "Israel." In Jack, then, we have a type of the whole House of Jacob, or the children of Israel!

When we hear the giant exclaim as he enters his house, "Fee, fi, fo, fum! I smell the blood of an Englishman!", we immediately understand that Jack is an Englishman. Here in this tale is the most direct reference to Israel as England that we have. Jack is very definitely an Englishman, or else the giant would have not sensed his presence in his house.

The Englishman today may be identified very easily. He has a cut, an air, that is quite properly his own. One can recognize him at a distance by his clothes, and by his language he is certainly known. We will not explore his characteristics in detail except to note here that an Englishman has a stamp which makes him different from all others. Although he was hidden, the giant knew that there was an Englishman present. Somehow, he knew!

We find another clue in the name itself, a name so familiar to the English, and so often used. The name "Jack tar" is so well known to us that we need no explanation that this refers to the English sailor. The Union Jack is likewise the name of England's flag. These simple usages of the name betray its derivation. Jack means Jacob and from this fact stems the whole plot of our story.

Therefore, the hero of our story is Jacob and every reference to Jack is not only a reference to Jacob, the man, but to Jacob, the progenitor of the "children of Israel" of the Bible. He is a type for the House of Israel, much as "John Bull" is a symbol for the English today.

Here, incidentally, is another clue to the identification of Israel with England. The bull was the symbol adopted by Joseph as the sign of his house, and it was displayed upon the shields and upon the standards of all who belonged to his house. There is a suspicion that he adopted this sign through his associations in Egypt, where the bull, or cow, was made an object of worship. He certainly was a man of high esteem in that country and the mother of his two sons, Ephraim and Manasseh, was a priestess in the temples of Egypt. Ephraim, the younger, has been identified with England and, as the receiver of the blessing together with his elder brother, Manasseh (the United States), retained the symbol of the bull as his own. The nickname "John Bull" for Ephraim's sons becomes, therefore, extremely appropriate.

In the Book of Revelation there is indicated a "place" to which Israel was to fly, the very same place called by Isaiah the "isles of the west"; namely, the isles of England and Ireland and the smaller islands near their coasts.

"And to the woman [Israel] were given two wings of a great eagle, that she might fly into the wilderness, into her place [the British Isles], where she is nourished for a time, and times, and half a time [1260 years], from the face of the serpent." (Rev. 12:14.)

With England marked as a future setting for the drama of the children of Israel, as indicated here in Revelation, we find a further identification of Jack as the Englishman of our story, and as the Israel of the Bible story.

It is probably for this reason that in this story Israel takes the form of a man, rather than that of a woman, as the case is in many of the other folklore stories, and in the Bible. The teller of the tale wanted, seemingly, to impart a direct truth, where there would be no mistaking the identity of Israel with England. It is the same truth that Isaiah and other prophets revealed in Prophecy, and which has since become a fact in human history.

In our story, however, Jack begins his adventures not in England, but in another land. As Jacob, the man of the Bible, the opening scenes place him in Canaan and Egypt. The story begins:

"A very poor widow once lived with her only son in a little cottage on the border of a great wood. They were so poor that often Jack went supperless to bed."

Anyone familiar with Genesis in the Bible will recognize this as descriptive of the condition of Jacob and his sons at the time of scarcity in the land of Canaan. Joseph, the son who had been left to die by his brothers, and was finally sold at the suggestion of Judah to a band of Arab traders, was now in Egypt. By his interpretation of Pharoah's dream he had been warned of God of the coming famine. Joseph, in storing up the grain, became not only the saviour of Egypt but the saviour of Jacob, his father, and all of his brothers:

"And all countries came into Egypt to Joseph for to buy corn; because that the famine was so sore in all lands." (Gen. 41:57.)

Very briefly, and in terms of symbology, the next sentence sums up the whole experience of the House of Jacob in Egypt:

"At last things became so bad that Jack's mother made up her mind to sell their cow."

The use of the symbol of the cow (Egypt) effectively typifies the term of enslavement in Egypt and the addiction of the children of Israel to the worship of Egyptian gods. So enamored of Egyptian gods had they become that at the time Moses was in the mountain talking with God they pooled their golden earrings and ornaments and melted them into gold to form a golden calf to worship. The symbol of the "cow" in the story speaks of the whole Egyptian experience of Israel and the adoption of many of the Egyptian ways of worship.

"On the way Jack met a man with a bag of beans in his hand. Jack took such a fancy to the beans that he begged the man to give them to him. [Evidently, the beans were very desirable to Jack.] 'No indeed,' replied the man, 'they are magic beans. But you shall have them in exchange for the cow.' To this the boy readily agreed."

How mindful is this passage of the promise of the children of Israel to Moses, "All that the Lord hath spoken we will do," the well-known vow made at the foot of Mt. Sinai. Upon this assumption, we shall perceive that the "man with the enchanted beans" represents Moses, and that the agreement he had with Jack (who is Israel) is none other than the covenant between God and His people. Take note that Jack wanted the man to give him the beans, but the man with the beans exacted the giving of the cow in return. This insistence appears to echo the verses at the beginning of chapter 20 of Exodus, when Moses came down to the people and spoke to them of the commandments of God:

"I am the Lord thy God, which have brought thee out of the land of Egypt, out of the house of bondage. Thou shalt have no other gods before me. Thou shalt not make unto thee any graven image, or any likeness of any thing. . . ." (Ex. 20:2-4.)

God revealed His plan for His people, but He required first that they give Him their entire attention and give up the worship of the cow of Egypt, a ritual which they found it difficult to part with. In return for this God made a promise to them through Moses:

"Behold, I make a covenant: before all thy people I will do marvels, such as have not been done in all the earth, nor in any nation: and all the people among which thou art shall see the work of the Lord. . " (Ex. 34:10.)

The gift of the magic beans betokens the many miracles which God wrought in bringing His people out of the land of Egypt and into Canaan. Not the least of these miracles was the precipitation of food in the wilderness of Sin, a food which took a small round form (suggesting a bean!), with which the children of Israel were formerly unacquainted. They gave it a name, "manna," and they ate it, together with the quail provided, and were sustained.

Also, "the people thirsted there for water; and the people murmured against Moses, and said, Give us water that we may drink." Moses, turning to God for an answer to this dilemma, was promised another miracle:

"Behold, I will stand before thee there upon the rock in Horeb; and thou shalt smite the rock, and there shall come water out of it, that the people may drink. And Moses did so in the sight of the elders of Israel." (Ex. 17:6.)

God performed many miracles for His people as they proceeded on their way to the promised land which was "flowing with milk and honey." Using Moses as His spokesman, God insisted that they keep their promise and make no more graven images of the holy cow of Egypt, nor the image of any other animal of the earth to worship.

Thus we find that the first few sentences of the story of Jack and the Beanstalk outline the early history of the children of Israel. It begins with Jacob in Canaan, extends through the bondage in Egypt and includes the return to the land of Canaan under the leadership of Moses, and the building of the city of Jerusalem as the capital of their new kingdom. Speaking to the people through His chosen prophets, God established them in Canaan, caused them to prosper and to prevail over all their enemies. It is a well-known fact to those who study their Bibles closely that, as long as Israel honored the covenant, God rewarded her and protected her from her enemies. But when the covenant was disregarded, to that degree God allowed her enemies to prevail against her.

We have identified just two of the characters in this story: but before continuing in this vein, let us look again at the story itself. Let us focus attention upon the miracle of the tremendous growth of the beans.

Jack went to sleep and while he slept they sprang up as a vine and made a fabulous ascent into the skies. As if in a dream, Jack went outside and started to climb the stalk, going higher and higher until he got to the top. This climbing of the beanstalk is emblematic of the very same ladder that Jacob beheld in his dream at the gates of Luz, where he saw angels "ascending and descending." Here different symbols are used, but the meaning is the same. This vision granted Jacob was but a prevision of the kingdom that God is to establish on earth, where men and angels will mingle on earth and have equal access to the secrets of heaven.

A casual reading of this passage of the Scriptures will not divulge the greater inner initiation which Jacob was given on that hallowed night. Jacob is here again but a type of all Israel and of all who overcome. Each in his own way, and according to the gift of God, shall experience this individually. In turn each of the prophets were given this same vision, and in the relation of their experiences we have in our Bible descriptions of God's realm which otherwise we would not have.

Collectively, this intimacy with heaven and the angels within it will some day be enjoyed by all. By this vision Jacob was shown the prospect of the Kingdom of Heaven as it would be established some day upon earth. He accepted the fact that this great event would come to pass in the far future; he was satisfied with the promise of God that through him and his seed God would make His Kingdom manifest upon earth.

Jack, symbolizing Jacob, aspired to this kingdom and began to climb the ladder. Yes, it is Jacob's ladder that he was climbing, the same ladder that is described in Genesis 28:12-15:

"And he dreamed, and behold a ladder set up on the earth, and the top of it reached to heaven: and behold the angels of God ascending and descending on it. And, behold, the Lord stood above it [at the top], and said, I am the Lord God of Abraham thy father, and the God of Isaac: The land whereon thou liest, to thee will I give it, and to thy seed: And thy seed shall be as dust of the earth, and thou shalt spread abroad to the west, and to the east, and to the north, and to the south: and in thee and in thy seed shall all the families of the earth be blessed. And, behold, I am with thee, and will keep thee in all places whither thou goest, and will bring thee again into this land. . ."

This latter promise was fulfilled when in 1917 General Allenby brought his forces against Jerusalem and England took possession of Palestine. In all other phases, the above promise of God to Jacob had been fulfilled. After the forming of a nation in the British Isles (land of the covenant, or brith), the English spread to all parts of the earth, north, east, south and west. The British Commonwealth of Nations, the United States of America, and kindred nations are the result of this promise. To say that these people have been, and are, a blessing to the earth in countless ways is a fact that history acclaims. As couriers of the Gospel alone they have fulfilled this prophecy. This missionary work has been going on for several centuries and today this work has been augmented by technical and economic help being given to the less fortunate areas of the earth. The assistance that the United States has given in food alone is too well known to enlarge upon.

After Jack reached the top of the beanstalk, "he found himself in a strange country," the story goes. "It appeared to be a barren desert; not a tree, shrub, house or living creature was to be seen." At this point of the story we meet the "little old woman in a long red cloak." Just as Jack spied the large house of the giant in the distance, this old woman suddenly appeared and told him of the nefarious nature of the odious giant. Jack learned that "his father had been wealthy and powerful, but his wealth and his good deeds had gained him the hatred of a wicked ogre. The ogre killed Jack's father and stole all of his money and some valuable possessions, one of them a hen that laid golden eggs, and another an enchanted harp. He intended to kill Jack and his mother too, but Jack's mother managed to escape. . . ."

In the above we are given several hints as to who the giant really is. We should first note the kind of country the giant abides in. It is desert country, suggesting the sands of Arabia that lie between Canaan and Babylon. The prototype of this "giant," who was to seek to wrest away the power and the very life of Israel, was Nebuchadnezzar. The actual image he set up in the plain of Dura was giant in size (Dan. 3:1). The order was given that all should "fall down and worship the golden image that Nebuchadnezzar the king had set up." (Dan. 3:7) It will be noted that, at the dedication of the image, all the "princes, the governors, and captains, the judges, the treasurers, the counsellors, the sheriffs, and all the rulers of the provinces" were required to be present. Having conquered all the civilized world of that time, Nebuchadnezzar sought to ensure the permanence of his victories by the establishment of a new religion and a new economy. Henceforth gold became the medium of exchange, and has continued to be so down to our present day.

It should be reiterated here that Jack represents Jacob-Israel, but as time elapsed his sons and their families multiplied so that, in the time of Nebuchadnezzar, the Israelites were a great multitude. Israel had been divided into the House of Israel and the House of Judah. The House of Israel was taken captive by the Assyrians in 721 B C and, when the Assyrians were overcome in turn by Nebuchadnezzar, we know how he went up against Jerusalem and took the House of Judah captive (604 B C).

The killing of "Jack's father," signifies, therefore, the capture of King Zedekiah and the attempt to end the reign of the House of David by the killing of Zedekiah's two sons. This passage is not to be taken literally, for it has no reference to Jacob's natural father, Isaac. It refers to an attempt to destroy for all time the reigning House of David. When Nebuchadnezzar killed Zedekiah's sons, he thought he had accomplished this. But he had not reckoned with the Israel law which allowed the transfer of title through the female members of the royal family; he had not reckoned with the daughter of Zedekiah, who was whisked away from Jerusalem by Jeremiah and brought, to Egypt. By this means God preserved the royal line of the House of David, transferring it by degrees to the northern shores of Ireland ; to Scotland and finally, to England.

"The valuable possessions" stolen by the giant signify the temple ornaments, the vessels and cups, anything and everything in Jerusalem made of precious metals taken by the Babylonians and set up in their own temples in Babylon:

"And all the vessels of the House of God, great and small, and the treasures of the house of the Lord, and the treasures of the king, and of his princes; all these he [Nebuchadnezzar] brought to Babylon." (II Chron. 36:18.)

"Jack's mother managed to escape," the story goes on to say. This may be taken as one of those living statements of truth, tucked away in the innocent composition of a children's story - a statement which Irish historical records bear out. One of the most dramatic episodes in Israel history is here hidden in the symbology of a Saxon folk-tale. And for what reason? Some ancient Saxon sage took this means of preserving intact, an ancient Israel truth.

In the sense that the House of David has been preserved and continues through the present reigning house in England, "Jack" has even now retrieved the "enchanted harp" which the giant stole from his father. The harp is, of course, the symbol of the House of David (I Sam. 16:19) and was taken from the house of the giant by Jack when he realized that it was his rightful possession.

However, the important detail should not be overlooked that the harp was not fully recovered by Jack until he had carried it down the ladder and had it safe in his home. This "home" is the same home that Hansel and Grethel tried to find after they left the witch's cottage. It refers to the Kingdom of Heaven of which Jesus so often spoke. The enchanted harp, then, will not be completely restored until that day when our Lord shall return to the earth and take His place, rightfully, upon the Throne of David. This event marks the ushering in of the Kingdom of Heaven upon earth. It is the time when "the God of heaven shall set up a kingdom, which shall never be destroyed: and the kingdom shall not be left to other people, but it shall break in pieces and consume all these kingdoms, and it shall stand for ever," as we are told by Daniel. (Dan. 2:44)

In the same way, a part of the material wealth that was stolen from "Jack" (Israel) back in the time of King Zedekiah has been restored. Responding to the obligation put upon His people Israel by God, England, at the time of the reign of Elizabeth I, began to enter into world trade and to prosper materially. Her ships were found on every sea. Commerce brought her in contact with every land. Her mind then became inspired with inventions, new ways of manufacturing, and she grew and prospered industrially more than any other country of the world.

But the giant is not dead yet! He is swiftly pursuing Jack across his threshold! It is not hard to see that the giant is hard upon Jack at the present time as we survey present-day England. Spiritually speaking, the nation is at a low ebb. It is an acknowledged fact that only a very small percentage of the people of England attend church. Economically, England has not yet recovered from the duress of World War II and the English pound has sunk to its lowest value on the world market. Food scarcities continue in a country which has always boasted of its table.

Starting with the attack upon Singapore in Asia in 1941, we have seen how the military power of England has been challenged and how, one by one, she has given up mandates and powers she had enjoyed for many years. The greatest concession was made to India; even now she is under pressure at the Suez Canal at the hands of Egypt and also in other parts of the African continent. Surely the time of "Jacob's trouble" is known in England today. But the time of trouble will come to an end and Jacob "shall be saved out of it." (Jer. 30:7)

In the second chapter of Daniel we read of the interpretation of a dream that puzzled Nebuchadnezzar. Daniel decribed four kingdoms which were to prevail in the world, starting with the rule of Babylon. He described this rule as a head of fine gold upon the "great image" which appeared to Nebuchadnezzar in the dream. Daniel made it plain that the Babylonian king was the first of these kingdoms and that the whole giant image, in all of its stages, would rule the world until "the stone that smote the image became a great mountain, and filled the whole earth." Here again is a picture of the giant with whom Jack has to deal. The day is nearly upon us when, like David of old, Jack will take up a stone in his sling and with it strike the forehead of the giant, and the giant shall fall down dead. On that day will be fulfilled all the words of the angel spoken to Mary, the mother of Jesus:

"And, behold, thou shalt conceive in thy womb, and bring forth a son, and shalt call his name Jesus. He shall be great, and shall be called the Son of the Highest: and the Lord God shall give unto him the throne of his father David: And he shall reign over the house of Jacob for ever; and of his kingdom there shall be no end." (Luke 1:31-33.)

The killing of the giant Goliath by David was, therefore, also a pattern of the future, and the stone in the sling is the same stone that will shatter the kingdoms of the earth. Jesus will come as He has promised and will be the "Capstone" and supreme Ruler of the Kingdom of God. Thus, the story of Jack, the giant-killer, is the story, not only of Jacob and the House of Jacob, but it is the story also of Jesus and His return to the earth. He will smite this giant who has falsely taken over rulership of the earth, and when the giant has fallen, the rule of the Kingdom of Heaven upon earth will begin. Our story again parallels the Scriptures when we read in Revelation 19:11-15:

"In righteousness he doth judge and make war . . . and the armies which were in heaven followed him upon white horses, clothed in fine linen, white and clean. And out of his mouth goeth a sharp sword, that with it he should smite the nations: and he shall rule them with a rod of iron: and he treadeth the winepress of the fierceness and wrath of Almighty God."

There is the third woman who figures in our story, she who lived in the house of the giant and befriended Jack, always warning him of the giant's approach and hiding him away. Who is this woman and what does she stand for in the world today?

In Revelation 11:3 we read of the Two Witnesses who are explained in verse four as "the two olive trees, and the two candlesticks standing before the God of the earth." To relate these two symbols to the symbol of Jack, the giant-killer, we shall arrive at an explanation of the woman in the giant's house. The two olive trees may be taken to be symbols of the House of Israel and the House of Judah, respectively. The Jack of our story incorporates both Israel and Judah as embodying the whole House of Jacob. The candlesticks are explained in Revelation 1:20 as the Churches, of which there are seven in all, each described in the second and third chapters of Revelation. The two candlesticks here stand for that purified portion of the Church which is blended with Israel and which shall join Israel in the rewards of the Great Day of the Lord.

The enigma of the woman who lived in the house of the giant is explained partially by the fact that she lived in fear of the giant and yet was friendly to Jack. When the giant was killed by Jack, we conclude that the woman was free of her fear of the giant and lived in her house in peace and contentment.

This woman can be likened to the candlesticks of Revelation, signifying the Church, a portion of which has succumbed to the power of the giant (Babylon, Mystery) and a part of which recognizes Jack (Israel) for what he is and is friendly to him. There are many in the Church today who would like to acknowledge openly the identity of the Anglo-Saxon-Israel peoples as Israel, yet are held back by their official positions.

The Church, in order to survive, has seemingly had to submit to the military and economic pressures of this great creature whose head of gold is Babylon. The Church has been linked inseparably with the wars of the princes of the earth since the days of Leo I (440-461 A D) when, as Bishop of Rome, he enjoined Emperor Valentinian III to establish a greater temporal power with the Church. Even the Reformation did not break this silent partnership. In England it was Henry VIII who needed more money for his wars and eyed the revenue that was drained out of England by the Pope of Rome for his own purposes. Luther would never have survived but for the friendship of the Duke of Saxony, who hid him from the ire of the Emperor Charles and, together with other Electors of Germany, backed the new movement with the sword.

The modern Church itself has acquired vast holdings and is burdened with possessions and "sayest, I am rich, and increased with goods." (Rev. 3:17) So Jesus described it. The possession of these goods exact an obligation from her, and so closely knit is the Church with the economic makeup of our times that she quite naturally responds to its requirements.

Modern business is based on contest, on conflict and upon the survival of the fittest. It is modified warfare, and it is only a natural consequence that war itself should burst forth in violent forms at intervals. History is punctuated with these adjustments between groups and between nations. Jesus said that man cannot serve both God and Mammon. When He comes in glory, it is a certainty that that part of the Church which is engrossed in possessions and the things of this world will not escape judgment. The true Church will be sustained and purified. That which is unworthy of His Church shall be taken away.

While Jack was in the giant's house he was befriended by this woman, who was interested in his safety, she herself being under the direct domination of the giant. We get a picture of a woman serving unwillingly, as a bond-slave. This woman represents the Church of today. She is partially in bondage to "the beast that . . . shall ascend out of the bottomless pit, and go into perdition " (Rev. 17:8), which, when it is killed, will free her from her bondage. In her desire to assist Jack we read in her a secret desire to serve God only, to be cleansed and purified, and to be found worthy and acceptable to our Lord in the day when He shall return to earth and the "two witnesses" shall ascend "up to heaven in a cloud."

Reading the eighteenth chapter of Revelation, we discover a parallel rendering of the death of the giant at the hands of Jack when, at the bottom of the beanstalk, he chopped through the stem and the giant fell to the earth dead. "Babylon the great is fallen, is fallen!" That the death of the giant-beast will affect the world's economic structure will be seen in the fact that "the merchants of the earth shall weep and mourn over her; for no man buyeth their merchandise any more." Then we will find that Jack shall have all of his money and his hen that lays eggs of gold, and he shall have his enchanted harp. He shall enjoy all of these things without further fear of the giant. He may join with John, the Revelator, in rejoicing that "after these things I heard a great voice of much people in heaven, saying, Alleluia; Salvation, and glory, and honour, and power, unto the Lord our God: for true and righteous are his judgments: for he hath judged the great whore [giant,] which did corrupt the earth with her fornication, and hath avenged the blood of his servants at her hand."

Wherwell, Hampshire
England

LITTLE RED RIDING-HOOD

Animals and birds have been adopted as symbols by nations from antiquity. The exact manner in which certain countries became associated with certain symbols is not always plain, but a few of them are traceable and are of importance to us as we study the symbology of the much-loved story, Little Red Riding-Hood. If we understand that the Saxon folk-tales are intrinsically messages to us in code, we must establish an index, or alphabet, by which we can decode the story.

England is widely represented as a "bull;" in cartoons John Bull, with the Union Jack as a vest, is the universal figure for Great Britain. From our study of "Jack and the Beanstalk" we have discovered the origin of this nomenclature, the bull, or cow, being the symbol for the tribe of Ephraim. Russia is a "bear," the United States has adopted the "flying eagle" in its heraldry, and we have since treated with the "lion" found upon the flag of Scotland, and also upon the royal coat-of-arms of the British monarchy, which stands for Judah and the House of David. There are countless references in the Bible to Judah as the lion, and Jesus Himself is referred to as "the lion of the tribe of Judah."

It is of interest to us here that John, in his description of his view of the throne of heaven, speaks of four beasts which were around the throne, "the first beast was like a lion, and the second beast like a calf (cow or bull), and the third beast had the face of a man, and the fourth beast was like a flying eagle." We have already seen how three of these creatures are adopted as symbols by two of the leading nations of the earth today. Is there some connection between these vibrant creatures that hover around the throne of heaven and the countries which have adopted them for national emblems? There undoubtedly is, but let it suffice here to note that the nations of the world are identified by certain symbols taken from the animal world. There are a few exceptions, the harp of Ireland being a notable one. The harp is an emblem, however, for the Throne of David; the original harp belonging to David being brought with Jeremiah as he fled with the daughters of Zedekiah from pillaged Jerusalem (580 B.C.). This telling symbol, proudly displayed upon the flag of Ireland, speaks more loudly than words of the role the Emerald Isle has played in the destiny of both Judah and Israel.

We shall focus attention upon one country, or one city, of Europe, to which a variety of symbols has been applied. There is the modern caricature of "the boot" given to Italy because its outline upon the map suggests a boot. Rome today is called the "City of the Seven Hills," a name which is as old as the city itself. It is by this characteristic that we find the city defined in the Bible: "The seven heads (of the beast) are the seven mountains, on which the woman sitteth" (Rev. 17:9). By this method may we identify the woman, "MYSTERY, BABYLON THE GREAT, THE MOTHER OF HARLOTS AND ABOMINATIONS OF THE EARTH," with Rome. In this chapter of Revelation the various natures of this "woman" are dealt with and, by a study of this many-sided creature, we find that "she" has a military, a political, an economic and an ecclesiastical make-up. In the drama of history she has played upon the stage of the world in all of these roles. We shall see in the story of little Red Riding-Hood how all four phases of Rome's power affect Israel.

We shall, therefore, look back into the very beginnings of Rome, to the legend of the founding of the city upon the banks of the Tiber, at a time fixed at about 753 B. C. The story of Romulus and Remus is too well known to dwell upon in full detail, but let us recall that one of the daughters of the royal house of Latinus (into which family Aenius of Troy had married) had twin sons. A tyrant king, who had usurped the throne, had the babes thrown out upon the banks of the Tiber. A she-wolf found the infants, carried them to a near-by cave, and nursed them. A shepherd named Faustulus came upon them, took them home with him and raised them to manhood. They overcame the usurper of the throne and set themselves up as rulers. To celebrate they decided to found a new city. In a quarrel over the site of the city Remus was killed and the site selected by Romulus on the Palentine Hill overlooking the Tiber was the one chosen. The city, of course, was named after him: it was called Rome. Thus Romulus, who was nursed at the teats of a she-wolf, was the founder of Rome, and the wolf has always been adulated by the Romans for the part it played in the origin of the city.

With this in mind, let us approach the story of little Red Riding-Hood. Next to the girl herself, the most prominent characterization in the story is that of the wolf, who meets her as she goes along the way to her grandmother's home. We get a picture of a guileless, happy girl, who little suspects the design which the wolf has upon her when they meet. We have already become acquainted with the little girls who **set off through the woods** in the person of Snow-White and of Grethel, and we have discovered in them symbols for **Israel**.

More properly, little Red Riding-Hood has the happy, laughing character of Isaac, whose name means "laughter." "And Sarah said, God hath made me to laugh, so that all that hear will laugh with me" (Gen. 21:6). Although little Red Riding-Hood inherits some of this happy, sunny nature, for the purposes of this story she shall be likened to the children of Israel, who set off so long ago on their journey through the wilderness to the "isles" of the west.

With the opening of the story, we find the mother of little Red Riding-Hood sending her off with a basket through the woods to see her grandmother. By the very nature of her journey "through the woods," we can identify the girl as Israel. But who is the mother in this new setting, and who is the grandmother? Their true natures will be revealed to us as we continue.

The story is almost too well known to recount. What child has not heard it at his mother's knee? The general appeal of this tale is unequaled in fairy lore, yet few there are who, hearing it, suspect the hidden message it contains. We shall touch upon such portions of it as shall give us a glimpse of its theme. Having decoded the character of little Red Riding-Hood as Israel and the wolf as Imperial Rome, we can readily see that the central theme of our story revolves around the relationship of Israel with Rome. Since the wolf was associated with Rome from the time of its very founding as a city, we can judge that this symbol incorporates all of Rome within its usage; the military strength of Rome is matched only by the development of her superb genius for self-government.

When these two aspects of her power became unbalanced and she fell apart politically, we meet up with a new kind of supreme authority that arose out of the ashes of the old, like the phoenix bird. This was the Rome that produced the Papacy and covered all of Europe ultimately as the Holy Roman Empire. Indeed, the symbol of the wolf embraces all of Rome, from its birth in 753 B. C. on the banks of the Tiber to the present day, as the story will disclose.

We shall not pursue here the history of Rome from its inception, but treat with it only as it affects Israel and her destiny. Let us go back only to the year 55 B. C. and look upon the land which the Romans had named Britania. Observe this far-off island and see the armor-clad legions of Julius Caesar as they jump from their boats and commence the subjugation of the island to Roman might. Why should Julius Caesar, already covered with glory by his exploits on the continent, brave the currents of the English Channel to pursue the glories of war in this far-away land? We shall find some of the answers as we study this innocent child's story and compare it with certain passages of the Bible and the prophecy contained therein.

To continue with history, Julius Caesar made two expeditions against the Celts, and conquered but a portion of the isles. This we may be sure of, the Celts made rebellious subjects, and during the next hundred years the Romans were too busy elsewhere to give much attention to them. It was not until the time of Emperor Claudius (41 to 54 A. D.) that legions were sent again to the Island. The Britons fought this time for nine years before they were conquered. Their defeat gave the Romans only the southern part, however.

It was Broadicea, Queen of one of the tribes in Britain, who precipitated the next war; this made the Romans more deeply en-trenched as masters than ever. Some Roman soldiers cruelly mis-

61

treated her and insulted her two daughters. Escaping, she drove her chariot throughout the land, calling the people together. Although the Britons fought fiercely, they were soon subdued. All who were not willing to obey them fled to the mountains, to join the Picts of Caledonia (Scotland) and the Scots of Ireland. From time to time raids were made upon the conquered areas, and to prevent these inroads into the country, the Romans built three walls more than seventy miles long across the island at its narrowest point. These were named for the three Emperors by whose orders they were built — Hadrian, Antonius and Severus. Along the walls at intervals were towers, where the Roman soldiers stood on guard night and day.

With this bit of history in mind, let us begin with our story. We find the mother calling to little Red Riding-Hood:

"Come, little Red Riding-Hood, here is a piece of cake and a bottle of wine. Take them to your grandmother. She is ill and weak, and they will do her good. Set out before it gets too hot. When you are going, walk nicely and do not run off the path. . ."

Compare this episode with the opening verses of Chapter 7 of Revelation:

"And I saw another angel ascending from the east, having the seal of the living God: and he cried with a loud voice to the four angels to whom it was given to hurt the earth (Rome) and the sea (the peoples of Rome), saying, Hurt not the earth, neither the sea, nor the trees, till we have sealed the servants of our God in their foreheads."

The servants of God in this passage are the children of Israel, poised and ready at the entrance-way to Europe. It was a great angel who was guiding them and protecting them, holding back the destructive invasions of Italy by the Goths and the Vandals until such time as the Israelites had safe-passage to Saxony, Normandy and England. The mother in our story can be associated with the great angel of God, sent to guard over Israel as she advanced through the wilderness of Europe to her destination. This great miracle of timing was witnessed by John as he beheld future events being revealed to him by the ascended Jesus.

The angel of God, seeing and knowing all things according to God's plan, knew that many of Israel had already arrived in Ireland and England. During the time of the bondage of the children of Israel in Egypt, she had watched the escape of many of the Zarah branch of the House of Judah to Troy, to Greece, to Latinus and to the isles of the west. This same protecting angel watched over the escape of Jeremiah and Baruch from conquered Jerusalem. Forced into fleeing to Egypt, they made their way together, accompanied by the ''daughters of the king'' (Jer. 43:6,7) to Ireland, thus carrying out God's plan that the Throne of David should have an heir. Without a doubt, this same great angel watched over the union of one of the king's daughters with a prince of the Zarah branch of Judah, continuing the royal line of David for posterity.

It is here that we find our clue to the identity of the "grandmother" to whom the mother sent her daughter with food and refreshments. Since the progeny of the marriage of Zedekiah's daughter to a prince of the Zarah branch of Judah caused the continuation of the royal line of David in the land of Ireland — and later Scotland and England — she may rightly be referred to as the grandmother of the kings of Ireland, Scotland and England. For it is through her that all who have sat upon the Stone of Scone have held rightful claim to the Throne of David, and it was to her that all Israel could give thanks for continuing the reign of David in their new homeland. During the time that Rome's military hold upon the island was weakened, the children of Israel began to arrive under the names of the "Angles," the "Jutes," and confederated tribes called the "Saxons."

The grandmother lived in a little cottage "out in the wood" and little Red Riding-Hood was admonished to stay upon the path and go directly to her. It is obvious that she didn't know what her grandmother looked like, or else she would not have been fooled so easily by the wolf. The symbol of the "cottage" is well established in Saxon folklore as meaning England and Ireland, both famed for their "cots." Hence we may deduct that, with the use of this strange imagery, the story of the migration of Israel is being retold — the escape from her place of captivity in Assyria to the land north and west: ENGLAND!!

"Just as little Red Riding-Hood entered the wood a wolf met her. Little Red Riding-Hood did not know what a wicked creature he was, and was not at all afraid of him."

It will be remembered that, by a series of questions, the wolf found out where little Red Riding-Hood was going. All the time eyeing her, the wolf thought to himself:

"What a plump mouthful — she will be better to eat than the old woman. I must act craftily, so as to catch both."

We are familiar with the part of the story where the wolf induced little Red Riding-Hood to go off the path into the wood in search of flowers, while he scampered to the grandmother's cottage. Pretending to be the granddaughter, he knocked, entered the door and ate the old woman up.

The eating of the grandmother is represented in history by the attempted conquest of England by Julius Caesar, an attempt to take by force the land destined to receive the children of Israel. The grandmother was a little hard to digest in the wolf's stomach, which is to say that, although England fell nominally under the control of Rome's military rule, she never actually reached Ireland or Scotland, nor did she thoroughly digest that part of England which she had gobbled up.

Ireland and Scotland, for over a thousand years to secretly nurture the throne of the House of David, were never actually subservient to Rome. The transfer of the Stone of Scone from Scotland to England by Edward in the year 1296 marked the final transfer of the House of David to its present resting place, London. "He cropped off the top of his young twigs, and carried it into a land of traffick; he set it in a city of merchants," as related by Ezekiel (Ez. 17:4). This transfer came at a time when all of the children of Israel had arrived in England and were ready to again unite into a nation and "a company of nations," as promised by God to Abraham so long before.

The next phase of the story marks another page in history. The wolf, having "eaten" the grandmother, donned her gown and cap and covered himself in her bed. Upon the arrival of little Red Riding-Hood (Israel), she was amazed to find the door of the cottage (England) open. Then began the famed set of exclamations made upon sight of the wolf:

"Oh, grandmother, what big ears you have!"
"Oh, grandmother, what big eyes you have!"
"Oh, grandmother, what large hands you have!"
"Oh, grandmother, what big teeth you have!"

At this point in the story the listening child was wide-eyed and expectant, but little Red Riding-Hood suspected that it was not her grandmother who lay in the bed. It is incongruous to believe that she was completely deceived by the wolf.

This act in the drama of Israel's adventure is reflected in the sending of Augustine to England in 596 A.D., a time when most of the Israelites had arrived on the English shores. The military power that was Rome's had given way to a new hierarchy of the Papacy in Rome. With the desertion of Rome by Constantine and the setting up of his throne in the east, the rulership of Rome was taken over by the Bishops. The temporal reins of government which had been with the Emperor now gravitated to the Bishop of Rome, who came to be known as the Pope.

With this change in garments (like the wolf who donned the night-gown), the greed that was Rome's reached out again for Israel and her habitation. In the person of Augustine, Rome reached out again toward England. Augustine was received in England not without much skepticism, and not without rejection. It is true that he won Aethelbert, the Saxon King of Kent, to his cause (597 A. D.) and with the King ten thousand of his subjects accepted the spiritual sovereign-ty of Rome and the Pope. Not versed in the facts, Aethelbert did not question the statement by Augustine that Peter had founded the church at Rome. He was unaware that Peter actually had been stationed in Babylon and probably had never seen Rome. (I Peter 5:13)

Aethelbert was so won over by the priestly costumes, and the appearance that Augustine and his fellows made, that he agreed to persuade his friends to the north into the new order. These were the Celts of the north, who had been Christians for hundreds of years before the coming of Augustine. There is today a famed oak in Worcester called Augustine's oak, which was the scene of his rejection by these wary prelates of early Christianity. Using tact, Augustine asked only three things of them in allegiance: first, that they should celebrate Easter in the Roman manner; secondly, that they adopt the Roman rite of Baptism; and lastly, that they join with him in the conversion of all the Saxons to the Roman faith. Upon the advice of a hermit, everything that Augustine asked was flatly refused.

But in their naivete these few Saxons of Kent had opened the way for the Roman Church in England. Little by little, England succumbed to this subtle influence from a foreign land. The culminating action was in 668 A.D. when Pope Vitalian appointed Theodore of Tarsus as Archbishop of Canterbury and ordered all services said in Latin. From that day onward, until the day of John Wycliffe, the Bible was a closed book to Englishmen in their own land.

This victory of the Roman spiritual regime in England is symbolized in our story by the eating of little Red Riding-Hood by the wolf — the wolf being "Rome" in a different garb. The climax of the story came when the wolf, who had eaten the grandmother, ate up little Red Riding-Hood, too. Just how the two kept alive in the stomach of the wolf is not explained, but they did! And this factor is eloquent of the status of Israel today — alive, yes! — but deep within the stomach of the wolf, as we shall see.

It is a matter of wonder to the child, hearing the story for the first time, that little Red Riding-Hood and her grandmother could remain alive in the stomach of the wolf. Equally so, it is a source of wonder that Israel and the Throne of David are in full existence in the world today. No wonder she has lost all memory, or consciousness, of being Israel!

In this connection it is well to consider the hood that little Red Riding-Hood was given to wear. A hood is a cloth-piece thrown over the head, oftentimes to hide one's identity. The hooded knight of old was one whose name was unknown, who often battled fiercely while incognito. In the art of falconry, it was customary to place a hood over the head of the falcon until the prey was spied, and then the hood was removed and the bird freed to fly to its mark. The hood, let us recall, was not worn by the maiden in the story until given her by her mother.

Thus, in the symbology of Red Riding-Hood, we find another of the characteristics of modern Israel. A hood is over her head. God made a promise to Abraham which was renewed with Isaac, and again with Jacob; this promise God intends to fulfill. But due to disobedience and the willful ways of the sons of Israel, they have fallen under the penalty of disobedience to the laws of God. One of these penalties was the loss of the knowledge of their origin and their destiny while enduring years of chastisement. Only today, after the passing of centuries of hardship and struggle, is Israel discarding her hood. One by one, those of Israel who are called and chosen and faithful are awakening and becoming aware of the rich heritage that is theirs in God.

Through our study of other Saxon folk-tales we have obtained vivid glimpses of the pages of Israel's history and we have seen how Israel made three separate attempts to lift the yoke of spiritual bondage placed upon her neck by Rome. The military yoke of Rome had been lifted when the Goths and the Vandals descended upon Italy and pillaged her cities, even the sacred city of Rome itself. It was in the interval that Rome's martial might was broken and the Papacy rose to power that the children of Israel passed safely over to England and settled there.

In hearty Saxon manner Henry VIII broke the religious ties that bound England to Rome, and in France it was King Francis the Fair who, in 1303 A. D., rejected allegiance to Rome. It was Francis who toppled the throne of the Pope at Rome and set up his own Pope in France, creating the first threat to the prestige and sovereignty of Rome in northern Europe. Finally, it was another Frenchman, Napoleon Bonaparte, who, in 1798, marched on Rome and took the Pope prisoner, thus marking the end of the political supremacy of the Papacy.

However, that other facet of Babylon's hold upon humanity — the economic aspect of this creature — is still present with us and its octopus-like grip has reached out to control every corner of the earth today. A description of this enslavement is found in the eighteenth chapter of Revelation. In this sense "all nations have drunk of the wine of the wrath of her fornication" and "the merchants of the earth are waxed rich through the abundance of her delicacies" (Rev. 18:3). There is no better description to be found anywhere of the state of the world today. War is indeed a lucrative business and the merchants in guns and ammunition, selling on all sides, are merchants of war and destruction — agents of Babylon.

In this respect Israel is still prisoner within the stomach of the wolf and seemingly there is no help for her. However, the story of little Red Riding-Hood had a happy ending:

"When the wolf appeased his appetite, he lay down again in bed, fell asleep and began to snore very loud. The huntsman was just passing the house, and thought to himself, 'How the old woman is snoring! I must just see if she wants anything.' So he went into the room, and when he came to the bed, he saw that the wolf was lying in it. 'Do I find thee here, thou old sinner!' said he. 'I have long sought thee!'

"Then just as he was going to fire at him, it occurred to him that the wolf might have devoured the grandmother, so he took a pair of scissors and began to cut open the stomach of the sleeping wolf. When he had made two snips, he saw the little Red hood shining, and then he made two snips more, and the little girl sprang out, crying, 'Ah, how frightened I have been! How dark it was inside the wolf;' and after that the aged grandmother came out alive also, but scarcely able to breathe."

In Saxon story form, here is another account of the First Resurrection (Rev. 20:5-6). We will readily recognize the rescuing huntsman as Jesus, the Christ, who knows well the machinations of His ancient enemy, "that old serpent, which is the Devil, and Satan," who, by His intervention, shall be taken from the earth and properly dispatched into "the bottomless pit." (Rev. 20:2-3)

"And the Lamb shall overcome them (the Kings who received power from the beast): for he is Lord of lords, and King of kings: and they that are with him are called, and chosen, and faithful." (Rev. 17:14.)

The entry of the huntsman through the door of the cottage can be likened to the imminent return of our Lord, as related in Luke 21:27:

"And then shall they see the Son of man coming in a cloud with power and great glory."

The knife, or scissors, with which the huntsman opened the stomach of the wolf can likewise be found symbolically expressed in the Scriptures. In the description of Jesus by John in the first chapter of Revelation, He is depicted as standing in a long robe that reached to the feet, and tied about the waist by a shining golden girdle. His face and His hair shone with the brightness and sparkle of the sun itself, and His eyes also sparkled as though afire. His feet, His whole figure shone out, ablaze with light, so bright that the eyes could scarcely behold Him. When He spoke to John, it seemed that His voice sounded sweet and rich and melodious "as the sound of many waters. And he had in his right hand seven stars: and **out of his mouth went a sharp two-edged sword!** " (Rev. 1:12-16.)

This word picture of the Master Jesus is, in its simplicity, one of the most eloquent descriptions of Jesus that we have. John was physically overcome and swooned at the feet of Jesus at the sheer power of His awesome presence. Such a vision as John had is a true vision of the cosmic Christ who, at His appointed hour, shall come to rescue His own. His words, at His coming, will lash out like lightning, free the overcomers from the fateful grasp of the beast (the wolf of our story) and raise them with Him into the glory of the resurrection.

Newton St. Cyre, England

SNOW-WHITE AND ROSE-RED

The test of true prophecy is quite simple. If history bears out the events foretold, then the prophecy made is true and acceptable. All of the words of the prophets in the Bible have proven true, even to the events leading up to our modern times. Many of the perplexities that plague us today as a people, and many of our mistakes as well, would be eliminated if we would give our attention to the prophets of Israel. The theory that modern man may stand apart from the prophecies of the Bible is a tragic fallacy, and an expensive one. Those who think they can read the Scriptures and skip the words of the prophets are making the same mistakes which were made by the Pharisees of old.

Much of the prophecy as given in the Bible is tersely expressed, and much of it is dressed in a symbology which veils its interpretation. This is due partly to the limitations of language. When a seer of Israel was given a vision of the future by God, there were no words to describe what he saw. Put yourself in the place of one of the ancient prophets. How would you describe to your fellows an airplane, a tank, a modern battleship or an automobile? It would be more than difficult; it would be almost impossible. It was only natural that these men resorted to parables and the use of symbols, to give their fellows an example of what was to come, of the things they had foreseen. Yet the remarkable fact is that they did choose symbols which would be easily recognizable by people of every language in every generation. They drew upon nature for their illustrations, and often chose birds and animals, for the characteristics of eagles, lions, leopard and bears do not change and are well known by all classes of people.

In the Saxon folk-tales we have a wealth of corroborative material on Israel prophecy. Many details are supplied about events which are previewed in the Bible. These details are for our information; they speak of today. If, as a people, we do not get these meanings from these stories, then we are not accepting our heritage as Isaac's sons (Saxons) and profiting by them. Israel of old was led by chosen men of God; as a nation her rulers were wont to listen to those holy men and to counsel with them on matters of national policy and decision. When it suited God's purposes, these men gave of their wisdom to rulers foreign to Israel, as witness the choice of Joseph by the Pharoah of Egypt for his chief counselor and the elevation of Daniel to a like position by the rulers of Babylon at a later date.

Today the United States and the other Western powers are in a dilemma. There is no Joseph or Daniel, and no Elijah, seemingly, to point the way for them in their contest with Russian Communism. Yet the situation today needs a Daniel and an Elijah to lead us successfully out of our difficulties. But, first, we must, as a nation, come to a conscious realization that we are a part of Israel, that we are Manasseh, the second tribe of the House of Joseph, and we share with Ephraim (Great Britain) the birthright of Israel. (Gen. 48:15-22)

With this full acceptance of our birthright, we must pay heed to the words of the prophets of the Bible, and recognize in Communism an ancient enemy of Israel. As a nation this enemy has appeared on the pages of history in many forms. It made its first appearance in the Bible in the valley of the Wilderness of Sin as the Amalekites, the descendants of a grandson of Esau, who opposed the children of Israel in their march to the Promised Land. How Israel prevailed against this foe is the subject matter of chapter 17 of Exodus. As a result of this threat against the throne of Jehovah, the Lord said he would have war with Amalek from generation to generation. (Ex. 17:16)

As the birthright nations of Israel, the United States and Great Britain are blundering along today; they are embattled with the forces of atheistic Communism, not recognizing their ancient enemy **because they do not recognize themselves!** Had the United States known this truth, do you think she would have been tricked in 1933 into the diplomatic recognition of the government of Soviet Russia? Do you think she would have allowed Russian embassies to be established in our country, each one of which has proven since to be a spy center? These and many subsequent blunders would have been avoided had she known the nature of her enemy.

In our treatment of the story of "Snow-white and Rose-red" we shall look for the appearance of a new actor upon the stage of Saxon folklore, one that has not been dealt with as yet. The tale parallels the Bible, particularly the events of the 17th chapter of Exodus and the 38th and 39th chapters of Ezekiel, commonly called the "Russian" chapters of the Bible. In these chapters America can be identified as "the land of unwalled villages . . . them that are at rest, that dwell safely, all of them dwelling without walls, and having neither bars nor gates." Great Britain is described as "the merchants of Tarshish, with all the young lions thereof." These nations, and others with them, are pictured as asking of Gog of the land of Magog (Russia): "Art thou come to take a spoil? Hast thou gathered thy company to take a prey?|" (Ez. 38:11-13) This manner of questioning implies a surprise attack; the two nations cannot conceive that this Russia, which up to a certain point had appeared friendly, will suddenly turn and attack them.

This is exactly the picture we get of the "bear" in our story as he pokes his nose through the door of the cottage, where Snow-white and Rose-red live with their mother, snug against the winter cold. The bear appears friendly and wants only a place by the hearth where he can get warm. The two girls and their mother let him in, and later we see him coming and going like a pet. Does this not coincide with the relations of the United States and Great Britain with the Russian bear, especially from the year 1933 to the present time? The "cottage" which the United States and Britain now share with the Russian bear is shifted to our own shores, to New York, where at the present time the UN is housed. But we are getting ahead of our story. Let us start at the beginning.

From the title we can readily see that our story is related to "The Story of Snow-white." Snow-white, as the herione in both stories, is Israel, but in the second story we are introduced to a sister, whose name is Rose-red. As the story opens we get a picture of a "poor widow who lived in a lonely cottage" with her two daughters, Snow-white and Rose-red. We are already acquainted with Snow-white, but who is Rose-red? As we know, the name "Snow-white" was derived from Isaiah who, in his first chapter, described the state of purity and perfection to which Israel shall attain in the latter days:

"Though your sins be as scarlet, they shall be as **white as snow.**" (Isa. 1:18.)

In verse 8 of his opening chapter, Isaiah refers to a **cottage** to which the daughter of Israel shall flee for refuge. Describing the judgment of God on Jerusalem and Palestine, he says:

"Your country is desolate, your cities are burned with fire: your land, strangers devour it in your presence, and it is desolate, as overthrown by strangers." (Isa. 1:7.)

Then, using the symbology of our story, he says, "And the daughter of Zion is left as a **cottage** in a vineyard." Why should the "daughter of Zion" be left, after the destruction of Jerusalem? This "daughter of Zion" can be none other than the tribes of Israel who wandered across the continent of Europe and built themselves small cottages in the faraway islands of Ireland and England.

We therefore surmise that the story opens in England rather than in Palestine. We can also see that our story is a sequel to the story of Snow-white, which began with the wanderings of the ten tribes after they left Assyria. If we can identify the sister of Israel, we can perhaps pinpoint the date of the opening scene in history.

The widow had "two children who were like the two rose-trees." One was named "Snow-white" for the white roses on one tree, and the other "Rose-red" for the red roses that grew on the other tree. Reference to the rose-**tree** here is very interesting as we often speak of the "family tree" in arriving at the descent of a certain family down through the years. The mother of the two girls is the trunk of this family tree, so to speak, and again we recognize her as one of the daughters of Zedekiah. There is here, an implication of royalty in regard to both of the sisters, since the royal line of the House of David was preserved through Zedekiah's daughter. We can thus identify Rose-red with the House of David and the House of Judah. Whereas, in the story of Hansel and Grethel, Israel and Judah were depicted as sister and brother, in the present instance they become sisters.

It was the marriage of this young lady of the Pharez side of Judah, with a prince of the scarlet thread, i.e., of the Zarah branch of Judah, that solved the riddle of the two ''eagles'' — a riddle that had been given out by Ezekiel for Israel to solve. (Ez. 17) This was the means chosen by God to preserve the House of David in compliance with a promise He had made to Israel and which He was bound to keep. That the vast majority, even in England, are blind to the fact that the House of David is today embodied in the present reigning House of England does not lessen its veracity, or its importance.

More exactly, history itself announces the presence of these two sisters in England. In a spirited contention of two of the leading houses of England for the throne, we learn of a war called the "War of the Roses." This war broke out in 1455 and lasted to 1485. The two houses in contest were the House of York and the House of Lancaster. The symbol for the House of York was the **white rose**, and that for the House of Lancaster was the **red rose**. While these two reigning houses of Britain cannot represent Israel and Judah directly, yet the presence of these symbols of the roses in English history links our story with England very definitely.

The clans of Judah, by the time they arrived in Britain, were known as the Jutes. The country took the name "England" from the Angles, or Engles, who were of the tribe of Benjamin. "Angeles" is the word for "messenger." It was the tribe of Benjamin that was singled out to carry the message of the Gospel to the Gentiles, and while a small portion of the tribe returned to Jerusalem, a larger number migrated with Judah to England, to give the name to that country which would later take the Gospel to all parts of the world.

England has indeed preached the Gospel to all the Gentile world. History proclaims that the Saxons were not just one tribe but, rather, a confederation of tribes. We know, of course, that other tribes of the House of Israel made their way to England's shores.

This story is of interest to all because it contains an account of the "guardian angel," an aspect so familiar in English art and literature.

"Once when they (Snow-white and Rose-red) had spent the night in the wood and the dawn had roused them, they saw a beautiful child in a shining white dress sitting near their bed. He got up and looked quite kindly at them, but said nothing and went away into the forest. And when they looked around they found that they had been sleeping quite close to a precipice, and would certainly have fallen into it in the darkness, if they had gone only a few paces further. And their mother told them that it must have been the angel who watches over good children."

While it is true that a particular office of the angelic host is the guardian of children, in this story, and on a national scale, this angel is the same angel who watched over Israel in England and gave protection in one of her greatest hours of danger. In the 10th chapter of Revelation this angel is announced as "another mighty angel . . . clothed with a cloud: and a rainbow was upon his head, and his face was as it were the sun, and his feet as pillars of fire: And he had in his hand a little book open: and he set his right foot upon the sea, and his left foot on the earth, and cried with a loud voice, as when a lion roareth.'" (Rev. 10:1-3)

When Elizabeth I took the English throne in 1558 A. D., she had a difficult task before her. Being a Protestant, she re-established the Anglican Church which had been quashed by her predecessor, Mary Tudor, a Roman Catholic. In collusion with the Pope at Rome, King Phillip of Spain tried by various means to recapture England for Roman Catholicism. Being rejected by Elizabeth as her suitor, he assembled the largest fleet ever built in the history of Spain and sailed out to take Elizabeth and England by force. The defeat of the great Spanish Armada is one of the marvels of history, and Elizabeth was the first to acknowledge God's protection over England.

The picture of this protecting angel having in his hand "an open book" — and a little book at that — indicated the printed Bible. Previous to the era of printing, the Bible had been copied by hand and was necessarily large and cumbersome. With the invention of printing, the Bible became a small book and was soon printed in great quantities. This bit of symbology bespeaks England's role in the spreading of the Word of God. With the efforts of John Wycliffe in the 13th century, England led the way in the translation of the Bible into the native tongue. By 1535 a complete translation was effected by Miles Coverdale, whose work was based partly on Wycliffe's and William Tyndale's translations. On the continent the hunger for the Word spread and Luther, Calvin and others made translations of the Bible into German and French. The fire of religious fervor was caught up in the great Reformation movement, which has since spread around the world.

In our story the experience with the guardian angel was followed by a picture of peaceful tranquillity:

"Snow-white and Rose-red kept their mother's little cottage so neat it was a pleasure to look inside it. In the summer Rose-red took care of the house . . . In the winter Snow-white lit the fire and hung the kettle in the wrekin."

The busy household activities of the two sisters suggest the busyness of England with building up her industries and her trade. She prospered under Elizabeth as she never had before. With the Bible being widely read, the ability of Israel to witness to God's blessings knew no bounds. The secret of this national affluence lay not only in the protection of the guardian angel but also in the willingness of Israel to go forth and preach the Gospel. The sun did not shine where you did not find Englishmen, and not only the colonist but the ship's captain too carried under his arm the "little book" — the Bible.

The esteem with which the English people looked upon the Bible is reflected in subsequent passages:

"In the evening, when the snowflakes fell, the mother said, 'Go, Snow-white, bolt the door,' and then they sat around the hearth, and the mother took her spectacles and read aloud out of a **book**, and the two girls listened as they sat and span. And close by them lay a **lamb** upon the floor, and behind them upon a perch sat a **white dove** with its head hidden beneath its wings."

Here in this passage we have the symbols of the Bible, of Jesus Christ and of the Holy Ghost, working together as a leaven which was meant to spread through the whole loaf, i.e., the world. Here, coupled with the reading of the Bible, is the descent of the Holy Ghost and the Spirit of Jesus Christ upon the reader, filling him with a desire to live according to the will of God and to follow His commandments. There is hardly a more peaceful scene than this in all literature, nor one which venerates more the nurturing strength to be gained beside the English hearth.

Then there was a disturbance, a knock upon the door, and "Rose-red, pushing back the bolt, met face to face — **a bear**! The bear began to speak and said, "Do not be afraid, I will do you no harm! I am half frozen, and only want to warm myself a little beside you!"

Here for the first time we are introduced to the symbol of the **bear**. If we comprehend the meaning of this symbol in all of its varied implications, we shall arrive at the meaning of a prophecy that will enlighten us on modern affairs. To begin with, let us search the Bible and see where we find the same symbol of a bear.

In the 7th chapter of Daniel the account is given of a dream Daniel had of "four great beasts, diverse one from the other";

"The first was like a lion, and had eagle's wings. . . And behold another beast, a second, like to a bear. . . After this I beheld, and lo another, like a leopard, which had upon the back of it four wings of a fowl. . . After this I saw in the night visions, and behold a fourth beast, dreadful and terrible, and strong exceedingly; and it had great iron teeth: it devoured and brake in pieces, and stamped the residue with the feet of it: and it was diverse from all the beasts that were before it; and it had ten horns." (Dan. 7:4-7.)

We are apt to think of the beasts in Daniel's vision as a reiteration of the Babylonian Succession of Empires as given in the second chapter of Daniel. To Nebuchadnezzar was given a preview of the seven "times" of Gentile rule, beginning with his own kingship and continuing into Roman times and beyond. But the vision given to Daniel was an explanation of **the forces at work inside of those kingdoms**, which extended on beyond the Roman Empire to our own times. Even Daniel could not quite grasp the whole meaning of the vision, for he wrote: "As for me, my thoughts greatly upset me, and my face changed color; but I kept the matter in my mind." (Dan. 7:28 **Smith & Goodspeed Trans.**) It appears plain that he could understand the nature of the first three beasts, but the fourth beast "which was diverse from all the others" greatly perplexed him.

To compare the fourth beast with just the Roman Empire is to fall far short in our comprehension of the scope of the vision. Imperial Rome has long ceased to exist as such and Papal Rome, as a political entity, has shrunk to the confines of the Vatican at Rome. Since we know that the Ancient of Days has not yet taken his place in judgment, as described in verse 18, we know that the ramifications of this mysterious "kingdom" exist in the world today and shall answer to judgment in the days ahead.

We cannot look for this beast of dreadful form, therefore, in any one nation today, but we shall discover it embodied in an international system of great power and influence, working through all nations without regard for boundaries or language. This was seen by Esdras in vision as an eagle:

"And I saw that all things under heaven were subject unto her (the eagle) and no man spake against her, no, not one creature upon earth." (II Esdras 11:6.)

This description of the sway of the eagle defines the secretive absolutism which holds in silence those men in high authority who could speak out, but fear to do so. Millions today, even the educated and seemingly well informed, live on in complete ignorance of this power gnawing at the vitals of their freedom; they little suspect the enslavement being planned for them. As foreseen by the Prophet Esdras, those who see and know, and could warn the innocent of these nefarious plans, are strangely silent.

Let us not confuse the symbols. The symbol of the bear represents but one of the several aspects of this hidden power in the world. Added to the rending power of the bear is the swiftness and cunning of the leopard, the strength and courage of the lion — all united and conjoined to make the fourth beast the most terrible and ominous of them all. The fourth beast runs rampant throughout the world today; his ugly body is sprawled across the globe.

It is the same beast mentioned in Revelation, which is to be bound and thrown into the bottomless pit. This beast is best described as a cruel, insatiable money system; it includes the satanic device of usury (interest) whereby whole peoples are laden with debt and the individual is almost completely occupied with keeping body and soul together and keeping a roof over his head. Answerable to this unseen power are the various governments of the world, and every senator, every representative, every member of Parliament knows it, but will not admit it. Its plans are carefully laid and secret, but the effects are apparent and widespread. It plays one nation against another, like chessmen, in order to gain its ends.

The nation which has so swiftly and recently emerged as a great world power is playing well the role of the bear. Her armies have taken Poland, Lithuania, Estonia and half of Germany. By the swipes of the Northern Bear's paw, either by force or by treachery, Czechoslovakia, Roumania, North Korea, Manchuria, Tibet and a part of Indo-China have been added to the list of satellites. Afghanistan is recently added to these.

It is obvious to all who are watching and alert that Russia, in her quest for power, most nearly fits the description of the bear as a part of the subtle, sinister force abroad in the world today. Just as the enemy of Israel, in her day of dispossession, was Assur, the same old enemy faces her today in new occidental dress. For the occidental spelling of the word, **Assur**, betrays Israel's enemy today: **Russia**! Interject an "i" in the word "Assur" in reverse and you have Russia! Using the cruel, Asiatic methods of conquest, even to the annihilation of peoples by transporting them bodily to Siberia, we can see that Russia answers well to the symbolism of the bear.

In our story the mother had sympathy for the bear, and called to the two hidden children, "Come out, the bear will do you no harm, he means well." That the bear was cordially accepted by the mother is something of a mystery to us here, yet might it not allude to inter-marriages in the House of David with the ruling houses of Europe and Russia? At one time the Czar, the Emperor of Germany and the King of England were all cousins. This would be on the positive side. It would allow for the attitude of the mother, who wanted her children to associate with the bear.

On the negative side this cannot mean anything but the gradual acceptance and employment by Israel of the Babylonian system of money and credit. Usury, a practice which King Alfred had vigorously outlawed in his day out of respect for Israel law, was practiced more and more in England. The breaking of this law of God alone has been the cause of much of the tribulation and sorrow that has come upon the Israel people. Whether they are in ignorance of or have disdained their origin, the fact remains that the Israelites entered into a covenant with their God, and as long as they break His laws, there will be a penalty for them to pay.

To continue with the story, the sister had three encounters with another strange creature, this time "a dwarf with an old withered face and a snow-white beard a yard long." As they went to the forest for firewood they came upon this dwarf, whose beard was caught in the crevice of a tree, "and the little fellow was jumping backward and forward like a dog tied to a rope."

Thinking what to do to free the dwarf, Rose-red pulled her scissors out of her pocket and cut off the end of his beard, causing the dwarf to rail at her for doing so. This part of the story coincides with that period in English history when Henry VIII broke off relations with the Pope of Rome and pocketed for himself all of the money that had been flowing toward Rome. It might well have been his boast that he "bearded the Pope!" Here, for the first time, we are introduced to a characterization of the Pope of Rome, and there is no mistaking him, for he carried a bag full of gold and precious stones. The Pope, as it were, got his beard caught in the crotch of a stout English oak; in getting free he lost part of his beard.

In Daniel 7:20 we can identify the Pope as a "horn" that came up among ten horns, "and before whom three fell; even of that horn that had eyes, and a mouth that spake very great things, whose look was more stout than his fellows." In our story also he has a definite role to play as it relates to Israel, and to the bear, as we shall see.

The children came upon the dwarf a second time, and on this occasion he had gone fishing and got his beard caught in the fishing line and couldn't get loose. "Just then a big fish bit, and the feeble creature had not the strength to pull it out: the fish kept the upper hand and pulled the dwarf toward him." Again the children rescued him. They tried to pull him loose but without success, so once more they cut his beard, much to the anger of the dwarf.

This fishing scene alludes to the attempt of the Pope to subject the English to Roman rule by inciting Phillip of Spain in 1588 to build his Armada and sail for England as aforementioned. However, as events proved out, the fish the Pope had on his hook was too big for him. In fact, this fish almost pulled him into the sea. The Invincible Armada suffered total defeat and again England had "bearded" the Pope. The use of the symbols of water, a fishing line, a hook and a fish clearly associate this passage with that period in English history.

There was a third encounter with the dwarf, this time when the mother sent the children on an errand to the town to get needles and thread, "and laces and ribbons." They had to cross a heath on the way to town and there they spied a large eagle attempting to carry off the dwarf. "The children, full of pity, at once took tight hold of the little man, and pulled against the eagle so long that at last he let his booty go. As soon as the dwarf had recovered from his first fright, he cried with his shrill voice, 'Could you not have done it more carefully? You dragged at my brown coat so that it is all torn and full of holes, you helpless clumsy creatures!' Then he took up a sack full of precious stones and slipped away again into his hole."

Here again we find a curious departure from the usual pattern of the Saxon folk stories. When in history did the English again come to grips with the Pope? It was not a direct contact. We will understand this if we identify the eagle which was attempting to carry off the dwarf. In 1796 a tide of war swept over Italy and the French general, Napoleon Bonaparte, crossed the Alps and defeated the Austrians, who had control of most of Italy. Napoleon established there the Kingdom of Italy, with himself as king. With Rome in his hands he took the Pope and threw him into prison. He claimed for himself the ancient powers of the Caesars. At his coronation his sceptre carried at its crest the golden figure of the Roman eagle and, as King of Rome, he can clearly be identified with the eagle in our story.

As a result of the battle at Waterloo in 1815, the English and the Prussians joined to crush Napoleon and break up his empire erected on the continent. The Papal states were returned to the Pope who, though briefly deposed, was reinstated. But the prestige of the Roman Church, the temporal rule that had been accumulated by the Pope, was definitely affected. Indeed, the dwarf had had many holes torn in his clothes, and he was ready to crawl into his cave again and rest for a while.

Thus we see what is so graphically enacted in fairy-tale form in the saving of the dwarf (the Pope) from the talons of the eagle (Napoleon Bonaparte) as the eagle sought to carry him away (had the Pope deposed and thrown into prison). While England had no desire to rescue and reinstate the Pope, she had the effect of rescuing him when she sought to squelch the ambitions of the French dictator, Napoleon, at Waterloo. It is for this reason, possibly, that the dwarf felt no particular gratitude to Snow-white and Rose-red for rescuing him, since he was rescued out of a sense of humanity by the two girls rather than for any other reason.

As the children were crossing the heath on their way home, the final incident occurred:

"They surprised the dwarf, who emptied out his bag of precious stones in a clean spot, and had not thought that anyone would come so late. The evening sun shone upon the brilliant stones; they glittered and sparkled with all colors so beautifully that the children stood still and looked at them.

"'Why do you stand gaping there?' cried the dwarf, and his ashen-grey face became copper-red with rage. He was going on with his bad words when a loud growl was heard, and a black bear came trotting towards them out of the forest.

"The dwarf sprang up in fright, but he could not get to his cave, for the bear was already close. Then in the dread of his heart he cried,

Dear Mr.Bear, spare me, I will give you all my treasures; look, the beautiful jewels lying there! Grant me my life; what do you want with such a slender little fellow as I ? You would not feel me between your teeth. Come, take these two wicked girls, they are tender morsels for you, fat as quails; for mercy's sake eat them!' The bear took no heed of his words, but gave the wicked creature a single blow with his paw, and he did not move again."

Needless to say, the above quoted section of the story involves us in prophecy, as the story relates to historical trends and happenings of a future date. This enmity between the two aspects of the Babylonian System symbolized by the dwarf and the bear points us to statements made in the 17th chapter of Revelation:

"And the ten horns which thou sawest upon the beast, these shall hate the whore (Mystery, Babylon), and shall make her desolate and naked, and shall eat her flesh, and burn her with fire. For God hath put in their hearts to fulfill his will, and to agree, and give their kingdom unto the beast, until the words of God shall be fulfilled." (Rev. 17:16-17.)

Certainly the Pope at Rome and the entire Roman CatholicChurch fiercely detest and fear the voracious Russian bear to the north. Russian Communism is a growing menace in Italy, for it is realized that with one swat of his paw, the bear could topple the Pope from his throne.

However, as our story approaches its climax, we find the characterization of the specific aspect of the bear merging into the larger interpretation of the Beast **System** and its political, economic, and ecclesiastical phases. In this respect both the bear and the dwarf may be considered as in the category of MYSTERY, BABYLON THE GREAT, THE MOTHER OF HARLOTS AND ABOMINATIONS OF THE EARTH. The heart of the system is its enormous wealth and a very substantial contribution to this is made by the material assets of the Roman Church, which are beyond calculation. The bag of jewels was most appropriate to identify the dwarf in our story with the Pope, for no collection of jewels and fine vestments can compare with the accumulation within the vaults (the dwarf's hole) of the Vatican at the present time. In the relationship of the Vatican to the whole Babylonian System, its economic power is more vital to the system than its ecclesiastical power, regardless of the fact that this is also very great.

Immediately after his final tussle with the dwarf, the two girls ran up to the bear:

"And when he came up to them his bearskin fell off, and he stood there a handsome Prince, clothed all in gold. 'I am a king's son,' he said, 'and I was bewitched by that wicked dwarf, who stole all my treasures. I have had to run about the forest as a savage bear until I was freed by his death. Now he has got his well-deserved punishment."

We become involved here in the highly-meaningful complexity of this unique folk story, the interpretation of which is no less intricate than the symbology of the Book of Revelation in the Scriptures. Undoubtedly, the author of the Saxon tale deliberately paralleled the Scriptural method of employing figurative language to conceal and at the same time reveal a hidden meaning. However, we can get our bearings here by referring to the 18th chapter of Revelation which deals with Babylon the Great. The shedding of the bearskin is simultaneous with the demise of the dwarf and the exclamation in Revelation 18:16-17 is applicable here:

"Alas, alas, that great city (Babylon the Great), that was clothed in fine linen, and purple, and scarlet, and decked with gold, and precious stones, and pearls! For in one hour so great riches is come to nought."

By the handling of its characterizations, our story subtly suggests that a terrific blow will be struck at the foundation of Roman Catholic power, which lies partly in its economic power. But further than that, in striking that blow, the Babylonian System itself will be utterly destroyed, thus setting the world free from its slavery, just as the "prince" was released from the bearskin. The righteous system will then be revealed by the manifestation of the person of the Prince, the King's son — who is Jesus Christ!

The righteous system, in its governmental, economic, and religious aspects, does not emerge from the Babylonian System, however. The righteous system was given to Israel at the outset of their establishment as the Kingdom of God on the earth at Mt. Sinai. But in succeeding generations, especially after their gentilization following their captivities and dispersal among the nations and the rise to power of the Babylonian Succession of Empires, there was a fast-growing incrustation of Babylonian influences which eventually overcoated their righteous laws with a hard shell of pagan practices (the bear's skin) never ordained or approved by God.

In the final struggle, the dwarf pleaded with the bear to spare his life and turn instead on the two girls:

"Come, take these two wicked girls, they are tender morsels for you, fat as quails; for mercy's sake eat them!"

This depicts the last desperate attempt to engulf the nations of Israel in the final destruction of the Wanton System. However, the restoration of Israel as a prince, ruling with God, is assured. This takes us back to the experience of Jacob at the Brook Jabbok, when he wrestled with the Angel in the night and his name was changed to Israel:

"And he said, Thy name shall be called no more Jacob, but Israel: for as a prince hast thou power with God and with men, and hast prevailed." (Gen. 32:28.)

Added to this is the fact that the Prince of Peace Himself shall intervene to save His people. We read in the story that Snow-white was married to the Prince "and Rose-red to his brother, and they divided between them the great treasure which the dwarf had gathered together in the cave." Compare the implications of the possession of the "great treasure" with the statement in Daniel 7:18:

"But the saints of the most High (resurrected and restored Israel) shall take the kingdom, and possess the kingdom for ever, even for ever and ever."

Compare also the reign of the Prince with the coming of our Lord Jesus Christ to take the throne of His Kingdom:

"I saw in the night visions, and behold, one like the Son of man came with the clouds of heaven, and came to the Ancient of Days, and they brought him near before him. And there was given him dominion and glory, and a kingdom, that all people, nations, and languages, should serve him: his dominion is an everlasting dominion which shall not pass away, and his kingdom that which shall not be destroyed." (Dan. 7:13-14.)

In the Book of Revelation the story ends on the same triumphal note, culminating in the marriage of the Lamb and His Bride — even Israel! The great marriage day of the Lord is the grand finale of the Bible and an invitation to the Supper with the Bridegroom, which precedes the wedding ceremony itself, should be the aspiration of every Christian. The calling of the guests to the Supper is still future, but who shall say how far future?

THE TWELVE BROTHERS

The Biblical image of Israel as a young woman is well known to students of the Bible. The Saxon folk-tales incorporate the feminine role for the heroine, Israel, more often than the masculine. Occasionally, though, we discover a departure from this pattern. The spinner of the tale of the Twelve Brothers dropped the role of a woman for Israel and spoke directly from the pages of Genesis in this tale. Certainly the saga of the twelve sons of Jacob is one of the most fascinating of any in Scripture. There is no subject in the Bible more essential to an understanding of the complex problems that face us today, as a people, making up modern Israel.

The creator of the fairy stories recognized this important fact. The story of the twelve sons of Jacob is the central theme of the Twelve Brothers and there is no disguise of this purpose. In this account Israel becomes not a young princess, but twelve princes! Here there is no chance of a mistaken identity. These twelve brothers are the twelve sons of Jacob who were singled out by God to become a great "nation and a company of nations." Our story does not give us all the names of the brothers, but we are given the name of the youngest, Benjamin! With this name as a clue we can easily guess the names of the others, beginning with Reuben, the eldest, and on down the list to Benjamin, the youngest.

Just as Benjamin is singled out in our story, Benjamin of the Bible plays a significant role. The special love of Jacob for Benjamin is shown in his reluctance to send him with his older brothers to Egypt for corn in the time of famine. Benjamin and Joseph were his only two sons by Rachel, the one who was closest to his heart. Upon the loss of Joseph Jacob clung closer to Benjamin, his youngest.

Benjamin was unique in the very manner and place of his birth. All of the other brothers were born at Padan-aram, which was to the north of Canaan, in the land of Haran. Benjamin's birth is distinguished by the fact that he was the only son born in the "promised land." Also let it be noted that Rachel gave birth to Benjamin near Bethlehem, the place God chose for the birth of His Son, Jesus Christ, at a later date. It is also highly significant that Rachel gave birth to Benjamin only a day or so after Jacob's encounter with the angel of the Lord, who changed his name from Jacob to "Israel," upon his way to revisit the site of Beth-el. It was here that "God appeared unto Jacob again. . .and God said unto him, Thy name is Jacob, but Israel shall be thy name: and he called his name Israel. and God said unto him, I am God Almighty: be fruitful and multiply; a nation and a company of nations shall be of thee, and kings shall come out of thy loins; and the land which I gave Abraham and Isaac, to thee will I give it, and to thy seed will I give the land. . . and they journeyed from Bethel; and there was but a little way to come to Ephraith and Rachel travailed, and she had hard labor. And it came to pass, when she was in hard labor, that the mid-wife said unto her, Fear not; thou shalt have this son also. (Besides Joseph.) And it came to pass, as her soul was departing (for she died) that she called him Ben-oni; but his father called him Benjamin." (the son of his right hand – Gen. 35:9-16.)

Born on the edge of Bethlehem we can see indicated the role which the descendants of Benjamin would play in the dissemination of the Gospel to the world. By his very place of birth it can be seen that Benjamin and his progeny were prededicated to the spreading of the Gospel. Because the Galileans, to whom Jesus chose to go for His Apostles and for His preaching and healing, were special people to the Lord is a fact which Scripture and history bears out.

Let us remember that those of Benjamin were separated and dedicated to the task of taking the words of Jesus and proclaiming them abroad. It was to Israel in the Isles (England) that "Benjamin" was commissioned to go, immediately after Christ's crucifixion, so that the story of the redemption of Israel should reach them without delay. Most of Jesus' disciples were of the House of Benjamin, with the obvious exception of Judas, who was of Judah. It was to these that Jesus spoke, saying, "Ye are the light of the world" and "These twelve Jesus sent forth, and commanded them, saying, Go not into the way of the Gentiles, and into any city of the Samaritans enter ye not: but go rather to the lost sheep of the house of Israel. And as ye go, preach, saying, The kingdom of heaven is at hand." (Matt. 10:5-7)

In the opening passage of our story we find that "Many years ago lived a king and queen who had twelve sons, all bright, intelligent lads; but they were not quite happy, although they loved each other very much. For one day the king told his wife that he had now twelve sons, if a daughter should be born, all the sons would die and their sister alone would inherit his kingdom and riches."

It is seen in the story that the king ordered twelve caskets for his twelve sons, in readiness for the future birth of his daughter. In his knowledge of the future the king takes on the character of God and anticipates the future happiness he will have with his daughter. It can be seen that the daughter of the king, the thirteenth child, is the shining symbol of a perfected Israel. In Revelation 12 we find a description of this woman, who has "upon her head a crown of twelve stars." She is personified in her role as Mary, the mother of Jesus. "And she brought forth a man-child who was to rule all nations with a rod of iron: and her child was caught up unto God, and to his throne." The resurrection and ascension to the right hand of God identifies this man-child. This story beautifully blends they symbols of Revelation into their historical outpicturing. It indicates the change from the Old Testament to the New Testament in the Person of Jesus Christ. And the vehicle for that change was Mary, the mother of Jesus. Therefore the death of the twelve brothers indicates the disappearance of the Twelve Tribes of Israel. But later they are to be resurrected by the power of Christ; what a lovely concept, which fits perfectly the Biblical story.

Let us remember here the important role of Benjamin. He learns of the coffins and wheedles from his mother the reason for their manufacture. Benjamin suggests that he and his brothers go away for a while and, at a distance, watch for the hoisting of a flag by the queen mother — a white flag, if the thirteenth child be a son, and a red flag, if it be a daughter. "Eleven days passed, and it was Benjamin's turn to watch. He saw the flag hoisted, and it was red — the signal that they must die."

The red flag signifies the shed blood of Jesus Christ on Calvary. This aspect of our story describes the banishment of the twelve tribes of Israel as voiced in the prophetic words of Amos, "Behold, the eyes of the Lord are upon the sinful kingdom, and I will destroy it from off the face of the earth; saving that I will not utterly destroy the house of Jacob, saith the Lord. For, lo, I will command, and I will sift the house of Israel among all nations, like as corn is sifted in a sieve, yet shall not the least grain fall upon the earth." (Amos 9:8,9) There is contained in this prophecy the destiny of the people of Israel, to be scattered among the nations of the earth. History reveals that they were scattered into new lands, where never man had lived before. Thusly the twelve brothers (Israel) escaped the penalty of death by flight, flight north and west from Canaan and from captivity in Assyria. The brothers felt that they must hide themselves, and this is born out in the story:

> "However, as they must still hide themselves, they went still further in the forest to find shelter. Strange to say, they had not traveled far before they came upon a most pleasant **little cottage** neatly furnished, but uninhabited."
> 'We will make this our home,' they said, 'and Benjamin, as you are the youngest and the weakest, you shall stay at home and keep house while we go out and procure food. . ."
> In this cottage they lived happily . . . so that the time passed quickly, but they heard nothing from home."

Here we meet again with the familiar symbol of the "cottage", which is identified with England and all of the isles known as the British Isles. In this part of the story we can see the emphasis put upon "Benjamin", who was entrusted with the spreading of Christianity in Britain, and from thence elsewhere to other parts of the earth. Our story reminds us that England has been the center of Christian mission from the very day that Joseph of Arimathea landed at Glastonbury and built the first Christian church there circa 38 A.D. Here again is painted the picture of the twelve tribes of Israel making their way slowly across the wilderness of the Caucasion mountains and following the Danube, the Rhine and other rivers to the English Channel and across the channel to England.

This "trek" through the wilderness, so definitely a part of the Saxon fairy tales, is predicted by the prophet Jeremiah to be means of grace to the wandering tribes of Israel. "At the same time, saith the Lord, will I be the God of all the families of Israel, and they shall be my people. Thus saith the Lord. The people which were left of the sword **found grace in the wilderness**; even Israel, when I went to cause him to rest." (Jer. 31:1,2) The people of Israel started a whole new life in the British Isles. It was a place where the grace of the Gospel was given to them and the past was forgotten and forgiven.

Again in II Samuel and I Chron. 17:9 we read of the provision of God for His people, in which passages God says, "Moreover, I will appoint a place for my people Israel, and will plant them, that they may dwell in a place of their own and move no more." This land was not Palestine, as many suppose. This land was a different land, where the scattered children of Israel were to gather and settle permanently. It was a land far from the oppression of Rome or any other nation. This land was England! The direction in which this land was to be found was indicated by the prophet Jeremiah, who said, "Backsliding Israel hath justified herself more than treacherous Judah. Go and proclaim these words toward the **north**." (Jer. 3:11-12) Isaiah was a little more explicit in pointing out the direction Israel should take in their migration to the north-west. "Behold, these shall come from afar: and, lo, these from the north and the west. . ." (Isa. 49:12) Through the leadership of the tribe of Benjamin the children of Israel were meant to adopt Christianity in their new homeland. After they had assimilated it they were commissioned to carry it to all parts of the world.

This commission was first given to Isaiah, who transmitted the message to Israel. God said to Isaiah, "It is too light a thing that you should be my servant, to raise up the tribes of Jacob and to restore the preserved of Israel; I will also give thee for a light to the Gentiles, that thou mayest be my salvation unto the end of the earth." (Isa. 49:6) This prophecy was fulfilled in history when Christian missionary societies were formed in London and in New York in the early part of the nineteenth century. The work of the English and American missionaries is a matter of record. The Bible was translated into many languages and given to people of all lands. These societies have translated the Bible into an estimated 1500 different languages, making the Gospel available to "the Gentiles."

Because of their disobedience the children of Israel suffered a period of punishment known in Scripture as the "times of the Gentiles or 2520 years. A part of the punishment was their forgetfulness of their true identity. Counting the passage of time from their being taken captive into Syria by Tiglath-Pileser III, 2520 years later the descendants of Jacob began to emerge into a period of blessing and power. This occurred in the early part of the nineteenth century. It is marked in history by the forming of the two great birthright nations, Great Britain and the United States of America. Biblically identified as Joseph and Manasseh. There is no other valid explanation for the sudden rise to power of these two nations, except that for the past 200 years the Lord God Almighty has carried out His promises made to them in the book of Genesis. Among the descendants of Israel these two brothers, Joseph and Manassaeh, have emerged as the leaders of modern Israel. They are the two birthright nations of the earth today.

To return to our story, the little sister, growing up, discovers twelve shirts in her mother's wardrobe and asks her mother whose they are. Discovering that she has twelve brothers who have gone away, she decides to follow them. Following them she "saw a light in a cottage, and stepped up to the door and knocked. Young Benjamin opens the door. She is elated to find her brothers and the result was that "she stayed with them for some time, and was a great help to the youngest brother in keeping the house clean and cooking the game which the others brought home."

This spirit of rejoicing seems best retained today in the English madrigals and in the glorious hymns that have evolved from Christian worship. These early English songs convey to all the feelings that came out of early Christians in England upon hearing the "good news" of the Gospel. The different clans of Israel, as they began to arrive on the islands after their journey across land and sea, settled down and hungrily adopted Christianity. They joyously set about the building of the Church, free from oppression or interference of any kind.

This purity of devotion was preserved in the British Isles for several centuries. The early church, known as the Celtic Church, thrived and grew. As more and more of the brethren arrived on Albion's shore they readily adopted the Christian religion, whose seed had been planted by Joseph of Arimathea in Glastonbury fresh from Palestine.

This story of the "Twelve Brothers" jibes so closely with the prophecies we find in the Bible and adds confirmation to the largely unwritten account of the wanderings of the Twelve Tribes of Israel from Palestine to their new home in the British Isles. Not only are the twelve tribes identified but the commission of Jesus to His apostles to seek out the scattered flocks, as they assemble in their new homeland, and to teach them about the new Kingdom of God to be established on earth: this is the added message we see in this story of Israel. This vision of the coming kingdom was given to the prophet Ezra for a vision to Israel and Israel alone: "For all of you, paradise lies open, the tree of life is planted, the age to come is made ready, and rich abundance is in store; the city is already built, rest from toil is assured, goodness and wisdom are brought to perfection." (II Esdras 8:52) The same vision was given to the Apostle John on the Isle of Patmos, the vision of the New Jerusalem, as recorded in Revelation 21. Through the impact of Christianity this vision has been enlarged and offered to all who accept the Lord Jesus as their Savior and their coming king.

Most of the Fairy Stories end with the words, "And so the Prince and the Princess were married and lived happily ever after in their kingdom." Ezra was given a vision which might well be the pattern for all these stories, "I, Ezra, saw on Mount Zion a crowd too large to count, all singing hymns of praise to the Lord. In the middle stood a very tall young man, taller than all the rest, who was setting a crown on the head of each one of them; he stood out above them all. I was enthralled at the sight, and asked the angel, 'Sir, who are these?' He replied,'They are those who have laid aside their mortal dress and put on the immortal, those who acknowledged the name of God.' And I asked again, 'Who is the young man setting crowns on their heads and giving them palms?', and the angel replied, 'He is the Son of God, whom they acknowledged in this mortal life." (II Esdras 2:42-47) NEB.

The story of the Twelve Brothers was written for children. Many who are adults who read it will toss it aside as trivia, figment of the imagination. But Christians who read it might remember the words of Jesus, "Except ye become as a little child, ye cannot enter the Kingdom." If we read this story with the simple wonderment of a little child, perhaps God will reveal some of His marvelous plans for the future for us.

THE ENCHANTED STAG

Symbolism is common to all parts of the Bible. By the varied use of symbols men of God have had a two-fold purpose. Either they use symbols to clarify a teaching, or they hide the truth to hold it for future revelation. In the present day we are privileged to gather the meanings which were buried deep in hidden language by the prophets of old. Hence, it is most important to the reader of the Bible to learn the meanings of certain symbols, especially those that relate to our times. The Books of Daniel, Esdras and Revelation abound in puzzling word-pictures, each awaiting a certain unfolding of history for their explanation.

By way of example, Daniel relates in his book a dream that was given him during the reign of Belshazzar, King of Babylon. Daniel depicts four beasts, each one representing a reigning king, only one of which had yet come to power, i.e., the king of Babylon. Only the passing events of history could clarify the true nature of the dream, for the other three powers had not yet manifested. And so, history has, by degrees, unraveled the enigma of the prophecies of Daniel and the other prophets of Israel.

One set of symbols which Biblical scholars are apt to overlook is the group of fairy tales preserved for us by the Grimm brothers of Hanau and Hesse, Germany. While some of the similes in these tales are identical with those of the Bible, others are quite different and further unravel the intricacies of Biblical prophecies in ways that no other literature has done. Except for certain passages scattered throughout the Scriptures and one passage hidden in the Apocrypha, (II Esdras 13:41-43) no explanation is given of the whereabouts of the ten tribes of Israel. After their capture by the Assyrian kings, Tigleth-Pilezer III and Shalmanezer, they disappear from the pages of history. This is as it should be, for this also is a part of prophecy and a part of Israel's punishment. She was to lose her identity but not her heritage.

But the stories of the Saxon mothers, as told around the fireside at night, have served to preserve a wealth of information on the true identity of the Israel people. In these tales, reported faithfully to us by the Grimm brothers, Israel is again and again identified as the Anglo-Saxon-Celtic peoples, who, escaping captivity in Assyria, went north and west through the "Gate of Israel" through the Crimea and southern Europe to settle in Saxony, Denmark, England and Scotland. A most fascinating commentary on this fact is found in the story of the Enchanted Stag.

The story is of a "brother and sister who love each other dearly," a familiar pattern in the sagas of the Saxons, (see the story of Hansel and Grethel); their mother had died and their father had married a woman who was most unkind and cruel to them" (see the story of Snow-White). They suffer hardship under the cruel stepmother and decide to "go out into the wide world" and fend for themselves. They wander for a whole day and sleep through a rainy night in the woods, and in the morning the boy awakens very thirsty. He found a brook and was just bending over to drink when his sister hears a voice in the babbling brook:

"Whoever drinks of me,
A tiger soon will be."

Stopping her brother just in time, the little girl urges her brother on.

Here we might pause to recognize the boy and girl as the twelve tribes of Israel, including Judah, for as we have seen in the story of Hansel and Grethel the better part of Judah accompanied the "lost" ten tribes of Israel on their trek out of Assyria to their new home. The boy, in this story, more properly represents all of the tribes of Israel, and the girl fluctuates in her role of Israel and a kind of guardian Angel, guiding the twelve tribes to their appointed place in the "isles." The father in the story is, in a physical sense, Jacob, who was the actual father of the twelve boys whence sprung the twelve tribes. Yet, he is also a symbol for God, the Father, who, like Jacob, loves His children and cherishes them in their special destiny.

The story introduces a new symbol, not even found in the Bible: the tiger. What does the stream of water stand for? And what is the meaning of the tiger that the boy might have been changed into? The author of the story had something definite in mind; no random figures these. Let us continue with our story and see.

When the children next approached a spring, the sister "heard in the bubbling spring the words:

Who drinks of me,
A wolf will be."

The girl, in the role of guardian Angel, draws her brother away from the spring and thus saves him the fate of being turned into a wolf. This incident has a close parallel in the Book of Revelation, chapter 7, verse 3, where we read, "an angel, having the seal of the living God: and he cried with a loud voice to the four angels to whom it was given to hurt the earth and the sea, saying, Hurt not the earth, neither the sea, nor the trees, till we have sealed the servants of our God in their foreheads" The four angels referred to here are the four angels of Rev. 8, who let loose four great disasters that swept over Rome, and Israel was allowed first to travel across Europe, to pass safely on to Saxony and to England, before the destruction of Rome took place at the hands of the Goths, the Vandals and the Huns.

As seen in the delineation of the story of Little Red Riding Hood, the "wolf" is the symbol for Imperial Rome, and is easily recognized as such here in our story of the Enchanted Stag. Just as indicated in Revelation, the children of Israel (here depicted as "brother and sister") pass on unharmed to the land of their destiny, the land of the red deer, or stag.

There are no deer to be found in Palestine, and certainly no stag. The stag a reddish-brown deer peculiar to Europe only. The word "stag" is derived from the Saxon word, "stigen", and gives us a clue as to the locale of the next stream to which the children now come.

The boy is now so thirsty he declares that at the next water he will most certainly take a drink. At this streamlet the girl hears the words:

"Who dares to drink of me,
Turned to a stag will be."

So on taking a drink of this water the boy was turned into a stag, and the girl is startled to see her brother a faun grazing at her feet. And here we come to the crux of the story, and the purpose of it is now complete. The children of Israel, now miraculously changed into the "enchanted stag", have lost their identity as Israel and are become another people — they are now become Saxons! No longer are they a Palestinian people, but a strange metamorphosis has taken place. Like magic, they become a completely new race — Saxons, Angles, Jutes, Celts, battling their way into Saxony, into Hesse, into Denmark, into England and Scotland. Only the little sister knows the true nature of the faun, until one other comes to hunt him, a king, but he never guesses that the stag he hunts is a young boy in disguise. There is no greater clue in the fairy tales than this one, as to the change of character of the children of Israel. As if by magic, they are changed from one people into another, and to all appearances, they are a new people entirely, "a stag"-people, people of Germany, Denmark and England, the habitat of the stag, even to this day.

In retrospect now, what does the "tiger" symbolize. There may be a play upon words here, between the Tigris River and the animal of our story, the tiger. Certainly the stream referred to is in the area of the Tigris and Euphrates Rivers, and probably refers to the Tigris. The word "tiger" is derived from the Persian word, "tighri", the animal inhabiting the eastern part of that country. In any event, the "tiger" in our story designated the country of Persia, which more anciently was known as Babylon, or Assyria, and is the same in meaning as the **lion** of Daniel 7:4, which has the wings of an eagle. The huge winged lions that have been dug up by archaeologists at Sargon prove them to be the symbols for ancient Assyria and were used largely to ornament the gates to Assyrian cities and their palaces. Plainly, then, the tiger represents Assyria and its ancient empire.

Israel was taken captive first by Shalmanezer II (858-824 B.C.)

and, finally, in 730 B.C. the last of Israel was removed from Samaria by Tigleth-Pilezer III. They were settled in the interior of Assyria "in Halah and in Habor by the river Gozen (modern Kizil Uzun) and in the cities of the Medes." This area is located on the northern slopes of the Elburz mountains where the river Gozan flows northeastward and drains into the Caspian Sea. There is a village on this river today by the name, Abhar, which is the modern derivation of ancient Habor. According to the popular belief, the Israelites mingled with, and were assimilated by, the Assyrians. According to the history books, they "disappeared" and became "the lost ten tribes of Israel." Our story, though treated as fable, is actually closer to the truth than the history books, which are supposed to be based on fact. The children of Israel did not linger in Assyria, but "they formed this plan among themselves, to leave the heathen population, and go to a more distant region, where the human race had never lived, so that there, perhaps, they might keep their statutes, which they had not kept in their own country. And they went in by the narrow passages of the Euphrates river. . ." (II Esdras 13:41-43)

In the simple parlance of our story, the little brother (Israel) did not drink of the waters of the first stream he came to, the Tigris and Euphrates sources, but held his thirst and traveled on in quest of other waters. He traveled north of Rome and the threatened interference of Rome to a third stream. This stream can be realistically pointed out as the Danube, for it is the easiest route into the hills and forests of northern Europe, and it leads to the native haunts of the stag. There he lived with his sister in a "little hut" in the forest. There is a very touching description here of the girl and the faun living together in the hut, she taking fond care of him, knowing all the while that he was really her brother. In this sense the author, or originator, of the fairytales might be associated with the boy's "sister" for certainly there is a clearly-defined comprehension here of the true identity of Israel. And so might all be defined who comprehend this truth. Israel is not what he appears to be, but a tell-tale hint is given by the symbology of the stag. The stag, derived from the hind, is the emblem of the tribe of Naphtali.

The stag is in common use in the heraldry of Germany, in England and all of the Nordic countries. In significant language the story is telling us that Israel lost the old identification when she arrived in northern Europe and took on a new garb, a new name, a new identity. How plainly it is put! And all wrapped up in the charming fantasy of a fairy tale! Who would suspect the truth to be hidden in such a wrapping? No one!

We need not recount how the king comes ahunting and, wounding him in the foot, follows him to the hut. There he finds the girl, falls in love with her, and marries her. Then there follows the episode wherein the wicked stepmother, who thought she had done away with the two children, learns that the girl has married the king and that the faun is unharmed in their castle (shades of "Snow-white"). This wicked stepmother is identical with the "woman" of Rev. 17, who "was arrayed in purple and scarlet colour, and decked with gold and precious stones and pearls, having a golden cup in her hands full of abominations and fornication, and upon her forehead was a name written: Mystery, Babylon the Great, the Mother of Harlots, and Abominations of the Earth." And this woman John saw as "drunken with the blood of the saints and with the blood of the martyrs of Jesus." This woman is none other than the Roman Church which, in the Iniquisition, sought to judge the true Believers and by every possible ruse to subvert them and compel them to submit to her will and her rule. The story of the demagoguery of this church is the story of the Holy Roman Empire, the unsatiated power of the kings aligned with the Popes, and of the Inquisition. The story of the struggle for freedom from this rule is the story of the Reformation, starting with Wycliffe in England, and flowering in the work of John Huss in Bohemia and Martin Luther in Germany.

The story ends with the king making a decision. The stepmother has sent her own daughter to take the place of the queen. The ruse works for a time until the king finally declares, "There cannot be two queens," and reclaims his true queen, the heroine of our story. The stepmother and her daughter are sentenced to die, "the daughter to be devoured by wild beasts, and the mother to be burned alive." How like the fate of the beast in Rev. 19:20, "and the beast was taken, and with him the false prophet. . . these both were cast alive into a lake of fire burning with brimstone."

To quote from the story again, "No sooner was she reduced to ashes than the charm which held the queen's brother in the form of a stag was broken. He recovered his own natural shape, and appeared before them a tall, handsome young man."

From this we can conclude an important bit of wisdom, which will parallel the Book of Revelation. Israel will not emerge in true outward identity until the "beast" of Revelation has been destroyed. Those of man who "seeing, see" and "hearing, hear" (Matt. 13:13) can understand who Israel is today. Jesus gave the reason for his speaking in parables. He stated to his disciples that they should be spiritually tested by their ability to look beyond the parables, the symbols, and understand the meaning of them. This calls for spiritual perception. Those who are blind to these truths will remain blind to them to the end of the Age. Then will the truth be revealed to all men, but then it may be too late.

In his ministry Jesus is constantly urging his followers to sharpen their perception, to dig for spiritual truths in the Scriptures, and to so order their lives that they would be ready to enter in through the narrow door of the Kingdom, when that door should be opened to them. He identifies the wise ones as the "wise virgins" who have in their lamps the "oil" of comprehension and understanding. Without this oil in supply even professing Christians would be found wanting and would not be ready when the Bridegroom comes.

The Enchanted Stag is an impressive, if enigmatic, contribution to the understanding of the identity of the Israel people. For those who are too blind to see it, there remains only the rewards of the blind. To those who can see it and accept it, there are the rewards that come to the illumined, the expectant, the believer. The fulness of these rewards can only be grasped with the coming of the Master Jesus, and when that time comes he will be ready to enter into our heritage as Co-heir with Christ.

Welford-on-Avon, England

94

THE FROG-KING

Few readers of the folk-lore of the Anglo-Saxon people realize that each of these stories was created for a definite purpose, and that this purpose is closely linked with that of the Holy Bible. Many of the stories were told with a moral in mind. A good example of this is the story of the "Fisherman and His Wife." There is a Christian precept contained within this story, which is the very heart of the Christian message. Jesus voiced it in this manner, "For what is a man advantaged, if he gain the whole world, and lose himself, or be cast away?" (Luke 9:25) And the parable which he gave of the prodigal son can be likened to the foolish wishing of the fisherman's wife, who in her greed for more and more possessions lost all that she had. The prodigal son, after a time of wasteful and riotous living, found himself eating the husks thrown out to the pigs. He found his great mistake and decided to return home and to the ways of his father.

Others of the folk-stories that have come down to us through the years are tales of the children of Israel, meant to preserve for us the memory of a precious heritage that lies latent within the Anglo-Saxon-Celtic and kindred peoples of the earth today. They precisely fill in the gaps in history. Veiled in the garment of children's fairy stories, they contain the truth of a great racial past. This past has purposely been veiled by the will of God, and the teller of these tales shares this purpose in the manner in which they are told. They are the lingual bridges whereby we may cross over into the truth of the whereabouts of the children of Israel in the world picture today. They have very carefully and artfully created in the fanciful forms that we recognize today as fairy stories, but they are also a means whereby we may trace the descent of the Anglo-Saxon-Celtic people as Israel from the time of their disappearance into Assyria in circa 740 B.C., to their reappearance, under different names, in central and northern Europe and the isles of England and Ireland at a later date. From thence these peoples have spread to the North American continent, to Australia, New Zealand, Africa, and to other places. The facts of this great pilgrimage is the marvel of modern history and the great providence of God is gradually being revealed in the preservation of His people, Israel.

This portion of the folk-tales that preserve for us this great racial truth will some day take their place as **historical record** just as definitely as they now serve as amusement and as moral instruction to our children. In this capacity they can rank as a "sequel" to those parts of the Bible dealing with the wanderings of the children of Israel. In their contribution to the moral fibre of our civilization, they already rank close to scripture and bear out many of the truths of Jesus, who taught in His day chiefly in the same story-telling manner. Let us, then, look at another of these tales that deal with the children of Israel and which combines within its text also much of the teaching of the Good Shepherd who came to lead His flock back into the fold of righteousness and truth.

This story of the Frog-King, another of those gathered for us by the saving effort of the Grimm brothers, is one of the lesser-known of the Saxon household tales. It is easy to see why this story is not as popular with us as others, as the imagery used in it is not so appealing or understandable to us. The idea of a frog who became a king strikes us as being far-fetched, perhaps, and we are not drawn to the idea until we study it, pry behind the symbols used, and have a scrutiny of the inner meanings imbedded within the very fabric of the story.

This story, in its opening passages, has an extremely idealistic setting. We are given a picture of a King surrounded with several beautiful daughters. All these daughters are beautiful, but especially the youngest. She is a shining jewel in her father's eyes. Yet none in the story have names, except one person called "Iron Henry," who is very much in the background. It is much easier for us to recognize the identity of the King than Iron Henry. He is the same father King who appears in many of the other stories, who in our Bible is called by Jesus, God, the Father, and elsewhere as God, Almighty, Jehovah, and Ancient of Days. To Moses He revealed himself as "I Am that I Am." We have already identified Israel as the daughter of the father in these stories, i.e., the daughter of God, the Father. She makes her debut in many ways, but here she is the youngest and the most beautiful, and very much in favor with her sisters and her father.

These varied forms in which Israel makes her appearance in the household tales correspond strikingly with the various kinds of womanhood she adopts in scripture. In Isaiah she is described as a "woman forsaken" of her father, as a woman put off. In the Song of Songs she is pictured as a young maiden anxiously awaiting the coming of her lover. Hosea gives another picture of her as an estranged wife, "she is not my wife, neither am I her husband . . . and she shall follow after her lovers, but she shall not overtake them; and she shall seek them and not find them: then shall she say, I will go and return to my first husband, for then was it better with me than now." (How similar to the cry of the prodigal son!) The love and mercy of God is shown in this message of God spoken through his prophet Jeremiah to Israel, "They say, If a man put away his wife and she go from him, and she become another man's, shall he return unto her again? Shall not the land become greatly polluted? But thou hast played the harlot with many lovers; yet return again unto me."

In Isaiah 54:5-6 we find another reference to Israel as a woman and we also find here a key to the theme of our present story, "For thy Maker is thine husband; the Lord of hosts is his name; and thy Redeemer, the Holy One of Israel (Jesus Christ) the God of the whole earth shall he be called. For the Lord hath called thee as a woman forsaken and grieved in spirit, and a wife of youth, when thou wast refused . . ."

We are first given a picture in our story of the young princess playing, "in the forest at the side of the cool fountain." This is a typical scene of a favorite young daughter living with her father and elder sisters under the most ideal circumstances and environs. This scene closely resembles that given us in the opening pages of the Bible, the picture of Adam and Eve enjoying their happy life in the Garden of Eden. But now, something happens to disturb the serene and heaven-like scene. In the garden it was the serpent that made his appearance. In our story, a similar misfortune occurs. Let us turn back to our story.

The young princess is sitting here by the fountain playing with a "golden ball," which she tosses into the air and catches with her hands. Then, this ball falls out of her hands into a deep well, a situation so typical that we need not dwell on it, except that it has a deep significance in terms of Israel and her tribal history.

First let us examine the symbolism of the "golden ball." It is the gift of a loving father to his youngest child, a token of his love for her and his interest in her. This ball has a specific meaning to us as a symbol. From subsequent happenings we discover that it is, in fact, a symbol for the covenant which God has established between himself and Israel. Its golden quality bespeaks of royalty, and also light. The children of Israel are often called the "children of light" in Scripture.

God had spoken to Jacob and said, "Arise, go up to Bethel, and dwell there: and make an altar unto God. . .", and after Jacob had gone and done as he had been told, in obedience, God said unto him, "thy name is Jacob, thy name shall not be called any more Jacob, but **Israel** shall be thy name: and he called his name Israel. And God said unto him, I am God Almighty, be fruitful and multiply: a nation and a company of nations shall be of thee, and kings shall come out of thy loins: and the land which I gave to Abraham and Isaac, to thee will I give it, and to thy seed after thee will I give the land." (Gen. 35:1-12)

God thus renews the covenant which He had made with Abraham and with Isaac and promises to Jacob and his descendants a most wonderful future. Much of that promise has been fulfilled, the "nation and company of nations" which God describes here we know today to be the United States of America and the British Commonwealth of Nations. In the promise that "kings shall come out of thy loins" we can see a fulfillment of this in history, as we know it. Most of the kings of Europe can trace their lineage, in some degree, back to Judah, the son of Jacob and progenitor of kings. Although Zedekiah is the last of the Kings at Jerusalem, through one of his daughters , the royal line has been continued unbroken to this day. To Judah, upon his death bed, Jacob said, "Judah is a lion's whelp . . . the sceptre shall not depart from Judah, nor a lawgiver from between his feet, until Shiloh come: and unto him shall the gathering of the people be." (Gen. 49:9-10) The very presence of the blazoned lion upon the national flag and the coat-of-arms of Scotland shows that the prophecy of Jacob is outpictured in the history of this country. And when the throne of Scotland blended and became one with that of England we see the joining of the "two sticks" of Judah and Ephraim, as prophecied by Ezekiel. "Take thee one stick, and write upon it, For Judah, and for the children of Israel his companions: then take another stick, and write upon it, For Joseph, the stick of Ephraim, and for all the house of Israel his companions: And join them one to another into one stick; and they shall become one in thy hand." The stick here is the symbol for the sceptre of the House of David, the ruling house of Judah. The joining of the sticks was fulfilled in history when in 1603 A. D. Queen Elizabeth of England died and James VI of Scotland, a Stuart, became James I and king of England. Although the two governments were not united until the year 1707, this ascension of James Stuart to the throne of England marked the uniting of the two thrones. This unity is displayed upon the present coat-of-arms of the ruling house of England today. Upon one side of the shield we see the lion, symbol associated with Judah for ages, and on the other side, supporting the shield, we see the unicorn (a symbol interchangeable with the bull) the adopted symbol of Joseph, and passed on to his son Ephraim. The presence of the symbol for the House of Judah and that of Ephraim upon the English coat-of-arms betrays too plainly the joining of the two sceptres as prophesied by Ezekiel many years before it occurred.

In chapter 19 of Ezekiel is given a parable of the lion's whelps taken into a pit, which is part of his lamentation for the fate of the princes of Israel (Judah). "Moreover take thou up a lamentation for the princes of Israel, and say, What is thy mother? A lioness? it became a young lion, and it learned to catch the prey, it devoured men. The nations also heard of him; he was **taken in their pit**, and they brought him with chains into the land of Egypt. . ." (Ezekiel 19:1-4)

The reference here to the "pit" in the land of Egypt has a direct bearing on our story. Ezekiel is showing here by symbol how Israel, and particularly those of Judah, are given to the practices of Egypt and the worship of the Mother of God, even though they had been delivered out of Egypt by Moses. The "pit" here mentioned is the symbol for the degenerate state of Israel due entirely to their lack of decision to abide by the laws of God. Moses, when he came down from Mt. Sinai after 40 days and 40 nights with God on the mountain was astonished to find his people again in the act of worshipping the golden calf of Egypt; not having heard from Moses the people had gathered together and said to Aaron, "Up, make us gods, which shall go before us, for as for this Moses, the man has brought us up out of the land of Egypt, we wot not what has become of him" (Exodus 32:1) Moses was in such a rage at the lack of faith by his people that he threw down the tablets containing the laws and broke them. Moses thereafter was constantly battling the moral weakness of the people, who longed for the soft, easy life of Egypt and the worship of the Egyptian gods to whom they had been drawn during their long stay there.

This tendency of Israel toward the lusts and passions of life is spoken of by Ezekiel as Israel "taken into the pit of Egypt." The deep pit at the end of the lower passage in the great Pyramid of Gisah is the symbol in stone of "the pits of Egypt," i. e., the lowest depths to which man can descend. Once fallen into this pit the neophite found no escape.

And so in our story we find that the young princess, in playing with her golden ball, lets it fall and it vanishes into a deep well, "and the well was deep, so deep that the bottom could not be seen." "And on this she began to cry, and cried louder and louder, and could not be comforted."

The covenant between God and His people Israel was broken when the people refused to listen to the prophets. Through His messengers God exhorted the people to change their ways and to keep His commandments. The words of Jeremiah in direful lament reflect the feeling of each of the prophets when he said, "And I saw, when for all the causes whereby backsliding Israel committed adultery I had put her away, and given her a bill of divorce; yet her treacherous sister, Judah, feared not, but went and played the harlot also." Jeremiah 3:8) Between 745 B.C. — 721 B.C. the House of Israel fell captive to the Assyrians, a part of the penalty for having broken God's commandments. A little more than a hundred years later, in 585 B.C., the House of Judah shared in this penalty for her failure to live up to her part of the covenant. She was taken captive to Babylon by Nebuchadnezzar and Jerusalem was razed.

In these two events we find the parallel to the passage in our story when the young princess (Israel) loses her ball (the covenant) and weeps that she cannot recover it. Although all of the twelve tribes of Israel are given a chance to escape the full punishment (the ten-tribed House of Israel in Assyria and the House of Judah and Benjamin in Jerusalem at the coming of Jesus) all continue to fail in meeting the requirements of the covenants. This is reflected in a later development of our story of the Frog-king.

God allows a pall of punishment to fall upon His people; the crying of the princess is but the lament of Israel herself when she is thrust out of Palestine at the hands of the rude invaders and forced into a foreign land to serve their victors as slaves. "Thus saith the Lord, Behold, I will sling out the inhabitants of the land . . . and will distress them, that they may find it so." (Jeremiah 10:18)

Now in the story comes the croaking voice of the frog, already familiar to us in other stories. We have found that this voice loud and croaking alludes to the voice of God. It is not to be confused here with the voice of the King, but rather, it represents the voice of God speaking through His prophets (the frog) to his chosen people, Israel (the youngest princess). In the story the young princess hears a voice asking, "What ails thee, king's daughter? Thou weepest so that even a stone would show pity."

Using Moses as His voice God spoke often to His people, especially during their many hardships in the wilderness of Sin. In chapter 16 of Exodus we read about the difficulties which are met up with and how "the whole congregation of the children of Israel murmured against Moses and Aaron in the wilderness: And the children of Israel said unto them, Would to God we had died by the hand of the Lord in the land of Egypt, when we **sat by the fleshpots**, and when we did eat bread to the full; for ye have brought us forth unto this wilderness, to kill this whole assembly with hunger."

This is but one of the many murmurings of the children of Israel against the will of God, as readers of the Gospel will attest. But God continues to express His wishes through the mouths of the different prophets. And Israel is constantly doubting and railing against these few men selected of God for their faithfulness, and always God is showing them that He is their God and that He will provide for them.

In the instance given above, where they were without food in the wilderness, the "Lord said unto Moses, Behold, I will rain bread from heaven for you; and the people shall go out and gather a certain rate every day, that I may prove (to) them, whether they will walk in my law, or no." It is a significant thing to us in our study of the story of the Frog-king that the manna rained down from heaven in the form of "small round balls." In the 13th verse of this same chapter it says that "in the morning the dew lay round about the host. And when the dew that lay was gone up, behold, upon the face of the wilderness there lay a small round thing (a ball) . . . and when the children of Israel saw it, they said one to another, It is manna: for they wist not what it was. And Moses said unto them, This is the bread which the Lord has given you to eat." We thus find in scripture a confirmation of the covenant with God in the furnishing of food to the children of Israel and the form in which it comes is identical with the "golden ball" which the youngest princess is given by her father. The symbol of the "ball" links scripture with our story and bears out our earlier definition of this symbol: God has a continuing interest in His children and urges them through miracles to have faith in Him and their mutual covenant. In the story, the golden ball is given to the princess as a token of love; she likes it, but treats it as a plaything, but when she loses it she becomes immediately unhappy and is eager and willing to listen to the frog who offers to bring it back up to her.

And so, Israel listens often to the prophets. With Moses it was God who "called unto him from out the mountain, saying, Thus shalt thou say to the House of Jacob, and tell the children of Israel: Ye have seen what I did unto the Egyptians, and how I bare you on eagle's wings, and brought you unto myself. Now, therefore, **if you will obey my voice** indeed, and keep my covenant, then ye shall be a peculiar treasure unto me above all people: for all the earth is mine. And ye shall be unto me a **kingdom** of priests and a holy nation."

Readers of the Bible are also familiar with the prophets who followed Moses, all of them messengers for God, voicing His desires to Israel. We will not digress here to delineate the messages of each one, but we will bring to mind how, finally, God sent His Son, Jesus Christ, in a final appeal. He sent Jesus to speak His Word, and He told in many a parable of the Kingdom of the Father and promised that by His redeeming blood this kingdom shall be given, even, yet, to the earth. So familiar were the apostles to the theme of the Kingdom that we find James and John vying with each other for the honor of sitting on the right or left side of the throne! To them the Kingdom was the whole sum and substance of God's promise to His people, and when Jesus told them that He was to leave them for a while, they were all curious and anxious as to when He should return and establish His Kingdom on earth. Before the time of Jesus' ascension the time of His return was not known to him, and so He told them, "not even the angels know the hour, or the time, only the Father." Yet, from a study of the Book of Revelation we find that Jesus, through His sacrifice for man, earned the right to the knowledge of the future, and He revealed the future to all in that Book who should be able to delve beneath the symbology contained and read the truth written there.

Through these simple stories, these children's stories, He has divulged the whole pattern of Israel's future. History bears out many of its prophecies; though some of it is still future to us, we may easily put our faith in its fore-tellings.

If we may take the word of Origen, the great Biblical scholar of the second century, we may believe that Christ, as the Word of God, was present in the sayings of the prophets beginning with Moses himself. To quote from the preface of one of his theological books, "Origen De Principiis", he makes these statements, "All who believe and are sure that grace and truth were obtained through Jesus Christ, and who know Christ to be the truth, agreeably to his own declaration, 'I am the truth,' derives the knowledge which incites men to a good and happy life from no other source than from the words and teaching of Christ. And by the words of Christ we do not mean those only which He spake when He became man and tabernacled in the flesh; for before that time, Christ, the Word of God, was in Moses and the prophets. For without the Word of God, how could they have been able to prophecy of Christ? And . . . it would not be difficult to show, in proof of this statement, out of Holy Scriptures, how Moses or the prophets both spake and performed all they did through being filled with the spirit of Christ." If we may accept the logic of Origen, we can more readily solve the enigma of the frog and his voice. In our story it is plain to see that the voice of the frog is in the voice of God incarnate in Jesus Christ; furthermore, that Christ, the Logos or Word of God, was expressed in Moses' messages to the people as it was through Isaiah, Jeremiah, and all the other prophets. The content, or plot of the story of the Frog-king, would seem to bear out the thought of Origen, as will be shown. If the frog had come but once to plead with the youngest princess (Israel) we could readily identify him with Christ or one of the prophets who preceded Him. But the frog pleads with her several times, indicating the countless times that God spoke to His people through His chosen messengers, the prophets.

"Be quiet and do not weep," said the frog, "I can help thee, but what wilt thou give me if I bring thy plaything up again?" Here the voice of the frog undoubtedly represents the speech of Moses, for God used Moses first among the prophets to bring His people out of the degradation of the "pit" of Egypt. Having brought them safely out of Egypt, God, speaking through Moses, tried to quiet His people and to assure them that if they would fulfill their part of a bargain, He would fulfill His part of the bargain. But God did exact a promise from them, and they too readily agreed to do all of the things He asked. "All the Lord hath spoken we will do," the children of Israel glibly promised to God before Mt. Sinai, and likewise the youngest princess promised that she would do anything the frog asked of her, "my clothes, my pearls and jewels, and even the golden crown which I am wearing," said the princess. This shows the high value the princess places upon the "golden ball," indicating also its spiritual nature, as she was willing to give up all she possessed to have it back.

The pact was made. It was a promise that reminds us of the pact the children of Israel made with God, and the pact was as lightly taken by them. Like children, indeed, they did not realize that in entering upon a covenant with God, that the obligation was equally upon them to honor the covenant and keep the commandments. Had the children of Israel taken the covenant seriously and lived up to it to the letter, without a doubt the Kingdom of Heaven might have been established upon the earth long ere this, and all the years of bloodshed, of human misery, of sickness and pain would have been avoided. It is quite certain that the tribes of Israel would have escaped the hundreds of years of punishment which they have endured, had they kept the covenant. But God's love is merciful, and in the unthreading of the story we shall see how He plans to release His blessings finally, though belatedly, upon the earth.

In the promise that she would do anything that the frog asked, the princess certainly did not take the frog seriously. When the frog answered her, "I do not care for thy clothes, thy pearls and jewels, or thy golden crown, but if thou wilt **love** me and let me be thy companion and playfellow . . . if thou wilt promise me this I will go down below, and bring thy golden ball up again," we recognize the Christ quality of the voice. There is a startling similarity of appeal for the love of His followers, when in the 21st chapter of John, verses 14 to 19, we read of Jesus' sudden appearance amongst His disciples, "after he was risen from the dead." He asks Simon Peter thrice, "Lovest thou me?"and Peter is quick to answer in the affirmative, three times, "Thou knowest that I love thee." Then, thrice given, the admonition, "Feed my sheep," followed by the exhortation, "Follow me."

We are also familiar with the scorn which Jesus held for the riches of men, for high office and for the crowns which they wore upon their heads. This quality is shared by all the prophets, especially Nathan, Elijah, and Jeremiah, all three of whom spoke the word of God to their king regardless of their personal safety. This quality was displayed in more or less degree in the lives of all the prophets, and was consummated in the life of Jesus Christ. When Jesus in the wilderness gave His answer to Satan, "Get thee behind me," He overcame the lure of all that this earth has to offer by way of possessions and high honor. Thus, in the answer of the frog to the princess, we recognize this same disdain for such things.

When she had received her "golden ball" back, the princess left the scene, and we picture the insistent frog, flopping awkwardly after her. We are intrigued with that part of the story where, the next day, the frog "comes creeping, splish, splash, splish, splash up the marble staircase, and when it had got to the top, it knocked at the door and cried, 'Princess, youngest princess, open the door for me.'"

Although this appeal expresses the desire of all the prophets that the people return to the ways of God, this passage has a direct parallel to the words of Jesus in Revelation 3:20-21. Jesus here has just finished speaking to the seventh Church (the Church of today) the church of the Laodiceans and says, "Behold, I stand at the door and knock: if any man hear my voice, and open the door, I will come in to him, and will sup with him and he with me. To him that overcometh, will I grant to sit with me in my throne, even as I also overcame, and am set with my Father in his throne." This passage in scripture unmistakeably identifies the frog as Jesus, the Christ. He is speaking to all here who are of Israel and also to all who have overcome, even as He overcame the sins of the flesh. But by and large, Israel is deaf to this knock at the door. She is deaf to the pleading of the Prince and is blind to His true self. She hears only a loud voice, which has no appeal, and will not open to it. Yes, like the frog, it is Christ who is knocking at the door of each one of us, calling us to overcome our reluctance to let Him enter, to answer to the offer of His love. It is the same voice that calls at the door of the princess and cries like the frog:

> Princess! Youngest princess!
> Open the door for me!
> Dost thou not know what thou saidst to me
> Yesterday by the cool waters of the fountain?
> Princess, youngest princess!
> Open the door for me!

The "frog" has been knocking at the door of the children of Israel for centuries, and for many years previous to the sending of His Son, Jesus Christ. The frog, as the Word of God, had been speaking to Israel through the prophets, those men selected of God to speak His will to His people. Then, in the next passage, the frog is clearly defined as the Christ, when the king discovers that his youngest daughter has made a promise and not fulfilled it to the frog. He asks the youngest princess, "What does the frog want with thee?" and the princess replies to him, "Ah, dear Father, yesterday when I was in the forest sitting by the well playing, my golden ball fell into the water. And because I cried so the frog brought it out again for me, and because he insisted so on it, I promised him he should be my companion, but I never thought he would be able to come out of his water! And now he is outside there, and wants to come in to me."

The answer the king gives to this confession describes the exacting of justice by the father, the same kind of justice any father would expect of his child. And so it describes also the requirement upon Israel that she shall live up to the terms of the covenant, else pay the penalty. "Then the king said, '**That which thou hast promised must thou perform**. Go and let him in.'" One is reminded here of the adamant decision made of God when He said to Jeremiah, "Though Moses and Samuel stood before me, yet my mind could not be toward these people: cast them out of my sight, and let them go forth." (Jeremiah 15:1) This was the judgment pronounced upon the House of Judah by the Lord, which judgment had already taken effect previously upon the House of Israel. This pronouncement began the "seven times" of punishment which were put upon Israel for her disregard of His Word. This punishment might have been mitigated had she listened to Jesus, His Son, whom He sent to the earth to redeem His people and lead them back into the paths of righteousness.

Jesus, by example, constantly referred to the Father when talking to his disciples and the people. "Your Father in heaven," He reminded them of constantly, and "your Father knoweth" were the words of comfort He brought. In speaking of them as His sheep, in Matthew 25:31-34, He speaks of the time when He shall come again "in glory, and all the holy angels with him . . . and before Him shall be gathered all nations: and he shall separate them one from another, as a shepherd divideth his sheep from the goats. And he shall set the sheep on his right hand, but the goats on the left. Then shall the King say unto them on his right hand, Come, **ye blessed of my father**, inherit the kingdom prepared for you from the foundation of the world."

Then follows the saying which might have come from the frog in our story: "For I was hungered, and ye gave me meat: I was thirsty, and ye gave me drink: I was a stranger, and ye took me in. Naked, and ye clothed me. . ." For at the insistence of her father, the king, the younger princess opened the door and let the frog in. But she did not let the frog in gladly. There was rebelliousness in the youngest princess. She shared her food with the frog. When, by command of the king, the frog was lifted up to the table with the princess, the frog said, "Now push thy little golden plate nearer to me that we may eat together. She did this, but is was easy to see that she did not do it willingly." Then the frog becomes tired and asks to be taken into the princess' bedroom where he might lie upon her "little silken bed." Angry and infuriated the young princess takes "him up and threw him with all her might against the wall. 'Now, thou wilt be quiet, odious frog,' she said." With this action she thought she had gotten rid of the frog. She thought she had killed the frog. (So did the high priests of Jerusalem think to destroy Christ by having him crucified!) But no! "When he fell down he was not a frog but a king's son with beautiful, kind eyes. He **by her father's will** was now her dear companion and husband."

This miraculous change of the frog into a "king's son" is synonymous with the resurrection of Jesus and His brief return into the lives of His followers just before the time of His ascension into heaven. Those first few followers of Jesus, whose eyes were open to His true nature, and the countless host of men and women who have been martyred for their glimpse of the true form of the Master, are those of Israel whom we call the "saints" and have accepted the Christ. Their physical lives have been given gladly as a sacrifice. They are the ones Jesus called to overcome, even as He overcame. They have earned their place in the Kingdom that shall be established soon upon earth.

But there are many of Israel alive upon the earth today who shall be called to join with these in the celebration of the great "marriage day" with the king. In the story we read that the King tells the youngest princess and her royal groom "that tomorrow they would go together into his kingdom." This promise is identical with the one made by Jesus, cited above, concerning His Kingdom, and the separation of the sheep from the goats at the time of judgment. The mention of a "tomorrow" in our story suggests an interval of time passing from the recognition of the prince until the time that Israel shall join Him and go into His Father's Kingdom. This interval in the story is the interval between the first advent of our Lord and His second advent, when the cry shall ring out, "Behold, the bridegroom cometh." (Matthew 25:6) According to the message of the parable of the "ten virgins" only about half of those who waited will be prepared for His coming. In Matthew 24:42 Jesus gives warning to the watchers, "Watch, therefore: for ye know not what hour your Lord doth come." And again, in verse 44, "Therefore be ye also ready: for in such an hour as ye think not the Son of Man cometh."

There are many in the world today who have lost faith in the coming of the Christ. Countless Christians have no acceptance of the angels and the words which they spoke to the disciples of Jesus who stood waiting and watching after His ascension on the Mount of Olives who said:

"Ye men of Galilee, why stand ye gazing up into heaven? This same Jesus, which is taken up from you into heaven, shall so come in like manner as ye have seen Him go into heaven." (Acts 1:11) But such was the promise, not only of the angels, but of Jesus himself. In John 14:3 He makes a definite promise to His disciples which has not yet been accomplished, "And if I go and prepare a place for you, **I will come again**, and receive you unto myself; that where I am ye may be also." Jesus told His followers that if He did not mean what He says He would not have said it. The same aura of wonder surrounds these words today as when Jesus spoke them nearly two thousand years ago, but if we are to believe all that He told us we must believe this cardinal promise of His second coming and expect Him.

The story of the Frog-king is the story of Israel. Part of the story is historical record. The balance is prophecy. The whole pattern of Israel's destiny is contained within it, just as it is hidden within the other Saxon household tales. The story deals principally with the reluctance of Israel to do the will of the Lord. The capture and enslavement of the tribes of Israel reflects the distaste which Israel had for keeping the laws, and also their distaste of the rewards of disobedience. Even crowded out of a place in history, as a "lost people" they had carved out a home in the wilderness and finally, in England, began to build up a culture based upon the message brought to them by Joseph of Arimathea, even the message of Jesus Christ. For Jesus had come upon the earth to live and to teach and to sacrifice Himself for **them** as much as for those of His flock in Palestine. "And I lay down my life for the sheep. I am the good shepherd, and know my sheep, and am known of mine. As the Father knoweth me, even so I know the Father, and I lay down my life for the sheep. And

other sheep I have, which are not of this fold, them also I must bring, and **they shall hear my voice;** there shall be one fold and one shepherd." (John 10:14-16) By a kind of racial instinct, in the manner that a sheep knows his shepherd, these people in a far off land heard and accepted the message of Christ as meant for them. Within the racial memory were strange stirrings at the words of Jesus, "If ye keep my commandments, ye shall abide in my love; even as I have kept my Father's commandments, and abide in His love. These things have I spoken unto you, that my joy might remain in you, and that your joy might be full. This is my commandment, That ye love one another, as I have loved you." (John 15:10-12.)

Many, in these latter days, are so deeply engrossed with the business of living their every-day lives that they do not look for anything else. The idea of a change of their lives, a set pattern, is disturbing. They like the idea of a Kingdom of Heaven on earth, but not just now! It might take them out of the comfortable groove into which they have settled. Yes, they go to church, some of them quite regularly, and they like to hear about the Kingdom but tend to hold the idea off from them with a long pole. The people and their attitude toward the promise of Christ, and the **asking** of Christ, are summarized in the characterization of the youngest princess in our story. The Christ, in the form of a frog, has no appeal for them. Many, in repugnance to the Word of God, have literally "flung the miserable frog against the wall" in hopes that they have killed him. But the time will come when He shall appear, when they least expect it, as the glorious Son of God. Ashamed and unprepared, these people will tragically repent of their disbelief and disobedience to God's word.

In terms of world events we are standing at the point of the flinging of the frog against the wall. There is an angel poised in heaven, "having the key of the bottomless pit and a great chain in his hand," who will come with the Christ and with "the armies which are in heaven" (Rev. 19:13-14) shall follow him upon white horses, and the Christ will be "clothed with a vesture dipped in blood: and his name is called the Word of God." Although this passage of scripture is still future, perhaps it will give us a clue as to who is "Iron Henry," the long-ago friend of the prince, who rejoices at the change of the frog into the prince. For in the conclusion of the story we find that the frog had been a prince before he had been changed into a frog and that Iron Henry had been his friend. We will not know until future events can verify it but Revelation would indicate that this friend of the prince is the "angel coming down from heaven". The name of this angel is given in chapter 12:7, "And there was war in heaven: Michael and his angels fought against the dragon; and the dragon fought and his angels, and prevailed not." It plainly states that this conflict took place "in heaven," and while this struggle is not a picture of the wars of the nations of the earth it names the great archangel who shall assist Jesus Christ when the time arrives that He should "smite the nations,... and rule them with a rod of iron." At that time Jesus shall have legions of angels at His command to do the work that will need to be done, and it is inconceivable that the Archangel Michael will not be close by His side in that hour.

Thurlstone, England

THE SEVEN RAVENS

A matter that is little understood in the world today, and especially within the Church where it is most needed, is the special relationship of Israel with the Church of Jesus Christ. This relationship is explained through the use of symbols in the Book of Revelation in the Bible. The symbols used are the candlestick and the olive tree. These are the two witnesses "standing before the God of the earth" as described in the eleventh chapter, and are to have an important role in the coming drama of the ending of the present age. It would seem essential that we have a clear understanding of the rapport of Israel with the Church, which shall raise them "up to heaven in a cloud", as further described in Revelation. This tremendous event is something that even their enemies shall behold, and for those of Israel who belong to the Church there should be something of expectation of these things that lie just ahead.

Our grasp of this is hindered, however, by a lack of understanding of the term, Israel. Unless we know who Israel is, we cannot know who it is that shall come to this reward. And the fact that Israel bears a common affiliation with the Church is the subject of not only the eleventh chapter of Revelation but of the story of "The Seven Ravens" also, with which we here deal. But first, let us look at the term, Israel.

As the Saxon fairy tales attest, Israel is discovered preponderantly among the descendants of the Angles, the Saxons, the Celts and the Jutes. Israel, as the name given to Jacob by God, is composed of the twelve tribes derived from his twelve sons, who in later years appeared upon the pages of history in the role of invaders conquering the island of England.

To understand the role of Israel, as it relates to the Church, it is imperative that we first determine who Israel is. Furthermore, without this understanding we cannot understand many of Jesus' sayings, particularly His promise to each of His apostles that each of them shall (in His future kingdom) rule one of the twelve tribes of Israel. It is obvious that since Judas betrayed his master that he shall not enjoy this privilege, but that Jesus Himself, as King, shall rule the House of Judah, together with the other tribes if Israel, in the fulfillment of His promise to the apostles. This was a definite promise made by Jesus and how can we know what He meant if we today do not know who are the tribes of Israel? If we do not understand this statement, how can we understand the angelic promise to Mary concerning her son, Jesus: that He shall sit upon the throne of David and that He shall reign in His kingdom upon the earth forever?

We have already seen how the stories that have come to us out of the dim Saxon past augment and amplify the meaning of the stories and the symbols we find in the Bible. With them we may unravel many of the mysteries of the past. We may also peer more confidently into the future. We know that God has a plan. The author, or authors, of these stories framed them upon a familiar Biblical background. We find old Biblical characters in new dress and in new surroundings, just as the children of Israel found themselves in new country and in new situations after escaping from Babylon. The new center of Israel activity had gravitated north and west to what is now Saxony, Denmark, Normandy and later to England, and finally to the Americas and to all parts of the globe. The very place of origin of these stories add another mark of identification of modern Israel. Conjoined as they are with the whole racial heritage of the Anglo-Saxon-Celtic peoples of the world today, their very content holds the key to further discoveries of this valuable heritage. They prescribe and hold the very birth-right of Israel, even though she herself has forgotten it. Someday, and soon, she will be glad to claim this birth-right! It will mean her very life, to regain it. But, now, let us turn to the story of "The Seven Ravens" and look for the message it contains for Israel, as a people, and Israel as an **agency of rescue** to the Church.

In this story the teller has very deftly reached out for new symbols, and he does this for a very definite reason. His purpose here is to portray the truths of the Bible a little more colorfully, a little more convincingly with a special appeal to children. He is also intent upon depicting conditions today, so that we in turn will recognize them for what they are. In this story he describes the modern-day Church, using symbols just as accurate and just as telling as any in Revelation. In Revelation John is shown the Seven "candle-sticks" as the symbols for Christ's Church. In our story the candlesticks are changed to "ravens", and the negative account of the seven Churches of Revelation becomes the story of "The Seven Ravens." In Revelation John tells how he turned to see the voice that spake with me, and being turned, I saw seven golden candlesticks; and in the midst of the seven candlesticks one like unto the Son of man, clothed with a garment down to the foot, and girt about the paps with a golden girdle. His head and his hair were white as snow; and his eyes were as a flame of fire; and his feet like unto find brass, as if they burned in a furnace; and his voice as the sound of many waters. And he had in his right hand seven stars; and out of his mouth went a two-edged sword and his countenance was as the sun shineth in his strength." (Rev. 1:12-16)

This description of the ascended Jesus is one of the most magnificent which the Bible affords. At the sight of this majestic being it is no wonder that John was greatly overcome and "fell at his feet as dead." In such a manner must have Jesus appeared to Saul on the road to Damascus. Saul, because of the dark purpose of his journey and by the negative nature that was his, must have been stunned at the sight of the glory of Jesus even more than John, John who loved

Jesus all the days of His ministry and was very devoted to Him.

It is significant that John spies first the seven candlesticks with which the very presence of the Christ is merged. In the last verse of this first chapter is given the meaning of the candlesticks which John saw: "The seven stars are the angels of the seven churches: and the seven candlesticks which thou sawest are the seven churches." The symbol for the churches is, spiritually speaking, the candlesticks. The reason for the choice of ravens as symbols for the churches by our author is explained in the second and third chapters of Revelation. These chapters are devoted to describing the churches in future history, pointing out to John **the faults** and **the error** into which the Church is fallen in each era of the future Church. While these descriptions are given as messages from Jesus to the local churches served by John (the churches at Ephasus, Smyrna, Pergamos, Thyatira, Sardis, Philadelphia and Laodicea, all clustered together within a very small area of southern Turkey) Jesus was speaking in larger terms to the whole of His Church as it extended its life down through the avenues of the future. Having been given knowledge of the entire future at His ascension into heaven, Jesus here describes the frailties and weaknesses of His Church as it expands and grows. These are all human qualities, not of the light. They were anything but spiritual qualities, the qualities of the lighted candlestick. So the Church as the **Raven** is described in our story according to its **worldly characteristics.** The raven wears the blackest of the black. In a search for symbols our author obviously chose this bird for its complete blackness. This bird is in direct contrast to the selection of the "white dove" found in the story of "Cinderella" and the "white duck" in the story of "Hansel and Grethel." Whereas the white bird denotes always the presence of the Holy Ghost, the black raven would denote the absence of this same spirit.

The lack of attention to the Holy Spirit is characteristic of the Church of today. Healing, which is a function of the Holy Spirit, is almost absent from the Church today. That divine alertness, which is so necessary to meeting the satanic influences in modern life, and awareness of the sublime presence of God so vital to the spiritual strength of the Christian, is lacking. Jesus describes this church as "lukewarm," and says "go then, because thou art lukewarm, and neither cold nor hot, I will spew thee out of my mouth. Because thou sayest, I am rich, and increased in goods, and have need of nothing; and knowest not that thou are wretched, and miserable, and poor, and blind, and naked." (Rev. 3:15-17) If this be Jesus' analysis of the future church, let us study the story in hand and see what we can find in it for us.

Our story opens with the announcement, "There was once a man who had seven sons," and in-as-much-as these sons are later changed into the seven ravens of our title we may associate these seven sons with the seven candlesticks as being **the true Church,** the living body of the Christ. These seven sons are also the **Church perfected,** since after being wished into being seven ravens, they are changed back again into their original nature. Seven is also the number of perfection, so that the use of the symbol "seven" in this story has the same meaning that it has in Revelation, and elsewhere in the Bible. This change of form from Ravens into men will lend us some enlightenment on the function of Israel in her relationship with the Church.

As the story goes, we find the father wishing that he had a daughter and, finally, after much waiting he is blessed with one. We recognize this daughter at once, from our study of other Saxon folktales, as representing Israel. The joy at her arrival was very great, but she was "sickly and small and had to be privately baptized on account of its weakness."

"The father sent one of the boys in haste to the spring to fetch water for the baptism. The other six went with him, and as each of them wanted to be first to fill it, the jug fell in the well." When the boys failed to return with the water the father suspects them to have gone after game and in anger makes a foolish wish, "I wish the boys were all turned into ravens." And so they were!

Baptism is an essential ritual in the church, being the first step a Christian takes in joining the church. The struggle of the boys over the jug indicates a contention amongst them, and would indicate the contention that has existed within the Church over doctrine — especially over the rite of baptism. Jesus said to the woman of Samaria, at the well, "Whosoever drinketh of this water shall thirst again: but whosoever drinketh of the water that I shall give him shall be in him a well of water springing up into everlasting life." Water that we drink must first of all be pure. Water symbolizes, therefore, in our story, purity of heart. This purity of heart is a prelude to the visitation of the Holy Spirit, of God Himself, just as was demonstrated at the baptism of Jesus at the river Jordan. Water signifies the living presence of God as avowed earlier by Isaiah, "The Lord shall guide thee... and thou shalt be like a watered garden, and like a spring of water, whose waters fail not." (Isaiah 48:11)

Zealous as were the apostolic fathers of the Church, in trying to form the structure of the Church many differences of opinion sprang up. Points of dogma became points of division. And from the earliest days of the Church the manner in which baptism should be administered has been one of the chief causes for splits within the Church. The fighting of the boys at the well dramatizes this difference among the different denominations over the proper method of baptism, until the real meaning of baptism has been lost. "The jug has fallen into the well," indeed, and the seven sons have been changed into seven ravens.

The choice of the raven as the form into which the boys were changed has great import here. "Black as a raven," is one of our strongest expressions of blackness. This black is even blacker than the night, which is always shot through with blue and violet. Black is the complete lack of color, just as white contains all colors. In fairy stories the witch is invariable clothed in black, has a black cat as a companion, and travels chiefly by night.

As the Bible clearly states there are two forces in the world, the power of God and the power of Satan. Satan has the ability to appear in different forms, beginning with the temptation in the Garden of Eden when he came to Eve in the form of a serpent. In the beginning the earth was created out of light (Gen. 1:3) and throughout the Bible God and His Son, Jesus, are seen in terms of burning, blazing light. On the otherhand, Satan is associated with the darkness, as stated by Jesus at the hour of his betrayal. "Then said Jesus unto the chief priests, and captains of the temple, and the elders, which were come to him, Be ye come out, as against a thief, with swords and staves? When I was daily with you in the temple, ye stretched forth no hands against me: **But this is your hour, and the power of darkness** (acting)." (Luke 22:52-53) At this time Jesus acknowledged the power of the darkness and he declared the chief priests and the captains of the temple as agents of darkness.

As agents of God and as bearers of light the children of Israel are often referred to as "the children of light." They were chosen of God to live and conduct themselves in such a way that He could implement the light through them to the uplifting of the rest of the peoples of earth. "Ye are the bearers of light." This drama of struggle between light and darkness is the very theme of the Bible and in Revelation we see the heralding of a final victory of light over darkness.

It is only to be expected that the church should become the chief target for the forces of darkness, once Jesus had been crucified and supposedly gotten out of the picture. Jesus foresees this attempt and points out to the church of Pergames, situated "even where Satan's seat is," the danger. (Rev. 2:13) Jesus foresaw the same old leanings toward the doctrine of Balaam, "the same Balaam who taught Balac to cast a stumbling-block before the children of Israel." (Rev. 2:14)

In the church named "Thyatira" Jesus perceives the same tendency in the Christians of the future to succumb to the age-old influences of Jezebel. He calls Jezebel a false prophetess, given as she was to the worship of Baal. And so, by degrees, Jesus points out to John the assault Satan shall make upon His Church in the centuries ahead. He shows John the weaknesses, and the strength, of His

Church in its seven phases of unfolding. To each one He imparts some few loving words of admonishment. Would that all in the Church today might hear and accept this advice, flung to them across the space of centuries by their leader, even Jesus Christ, their Lord!

The change of the seven sons into seven ravens bespeaks the entry of Satan into the very sanctuary of the Church; using the powers of darkness he has sought to change the character of the Church, to undermine the work of Jesus and twist it into an instrument of his own power. How he has succeeded in doing this is a matter of observation, even for those of the Church of today.

These are only a few of the more obvious intrusions of Satan in the life of our day; they are proof that the Church is not sacred to this dark force. Most of the influences of this force, however, are more subtle and not so easily detected. There is a silent, unseen force at work, a kind of hypnosis which would lull and put to sleep the "Watchers" within the Church, the same force that put to sleep the disciples in the garden of Gethsemane so long ago. "Sleepest thou? Couldst thou not watch one hour? Watch ye, and pray, lest ye enter into temptation. The spirit truly is ready, but the flesh is weak." (Mark 14:37-38). Thus asked Jesus of his disciples in that dark hour. Such is the question that He asks of every Christian today.

As the father spoke the words that changed his sons into ravens, "he looked up and saw seven coal-black ravens flying away. The parents could not cancel the curse, and however sad they were at the loss of their seven sons, they still to some extent comforted themselves with their dear little daughter, who soon grew strong and every day became more beautiful."

Then follows, in our story, a very revealing statement: "For a long time she did not know that she had had brothers, for her parents were careful not to mention them before her..."

This passage refers to a definite time - period in history. The little daughter we recognize again as Israel, the darling of her father's heart, (none other than God the Father, whose love for Israel is so variously expressed in the passages of the Bible.)

Latter-day Israel was ready when the first Christians began to arrive in Ireland, England and Scotland. In about the year 38 A.D. Joseph of Arimathea left Jerusalem and with a group of other followers of Jesus arrived on England's shores. They came inland to an island called Glastonbury and there he erected a little wattle church, the first Christian Church in England. Thus the seed of the Church was sown in England direct from Jerusalem by those who knew and loved Jesus. The Church grew and expanded, extending from England to Ireland and from Ireland to Scotland, so that by the time that the Angles and Saxons and Jutes began to arrive in England missionaries were sent among them to convert them to Christianity.

Chief among these Celtic Christians was Aidan, a product of the tiny island monastary of Iona off the coast of Scotland. Aiden wandered through England bringing the message of the Gospel to the invaders wherever he found them and singly converted more to Christianity than any other missionary. Thus was enacted the first meeting of Israel with the Church and the process of amalgamation began.

Thus, for this period of approximately four hundred and fifty years Israel wandered through the "wildernesses" of Europe like "lost sheep", unaware that their shepherd had appeared in far-away-and forgotten Palestine. Under penalty of God's law, they were sentenced to wandering without leadership, without their shepherd, and seemingly outside of God's grace.

But God, in His great wisdom, had sent Jeremiah in 580 B.C. with the daughter of King Zedekiah, to the "Isles" in anticipation of His "planting and building" the British nation and empire. In this way He sought to preserve the ruling house of David for Israel, this same Israel that was taken captive by the Assyrians and only beginning to break her bonds. Then in 38 A.D. with the arrival of Joseph of Arimathea on England's shores with the nucleus of the Church and the message of His Son, the time was come for **Israel's redemption.** And Israel answered readily to the call, to Christ.

This portion of our story points, then, to the period of history when Israel was "lost in the wilderness" and was ignorant of the existance of Christ and the birth of His Church. This is the period referred to by the prophet Hosea when he said, "For the children of Israel shall abide many days (years) without a king, and without a prince, and without a sacrifice, and without an image, and without an ephod, and without a teraphin." (Hosea 3:4). This was part of the punishment for having forsaken the laws of God. This punishment was not to be fully lifted from them until the end of the "seven times" of the Gentiles or 2520 years. The bringing of the Stone of Scone from Scotland to Westminster Abbey by King Edward signaled the end of the prophecy of Hosea and a prince of the house of David again ruled over Israel and no more would she be "without an ephod, and without a teraphim."

As the inflowing tribes of Israel accepted Christianity we witness the blending of Israel and the Church. This process was everwatched by an angel of the Lord, who says, in Revelation, "I will give power unto my two witnesses, and they shall prophesy a thousand, two hundred and threescore days (years), clothed in sackcloth. These are the two olive trees, and the two candlesticks standing before the God of the earth." (Rev. 11:3-4)

As was divulged in our study of the story of "Snow-White", the olive trees are the two houses, the House of Judah and the House of

115

Israel. Here is Israel pictured as **merged** with the Church, (the candlesticks) or a refined portion thereof, and readying herself for the coming of the Prince as a watchful, waiting Bride.

We get an idea of the function of Israel pertaining to the Church in a study of our story. The church in England was quite distinct from the Church in Rome, in Carthage, in Alexandria and in Constantinople, for it is linked very closely with Isreal. Destined to receive the restored rulership of the House of David, England became a chosen instrument for that particular purpose. Redeemed through the sacrifice, of His Son, Jesus Christ, the covenant relationship was restored and God began to use England as a part of His great unfolding plan for Israel and the earth.

This acceptance by Israel of Christianity and her new resolve is reflected in our story when the princess discovers that she has seven brothers and decides that "she must deliver her brothers. She had no rest or peace until she set out **secretly**, and went forth in the wide world to trace out her brothers and set them free, let it cost what if might."

While the early Church in England had thrived and in its zeal began to send missionaries onto the continent, the church at Rome was not asleep to the great field of opportunity that lay in England. Pope Gregory I sent Augustine as Archbishop to Canterbury. Acting under Gregory's guidance, Augustine sought gradually to make the English Church conform to Rome and Rome's requirements. He insisted on the use of Latin in the worship services, and sought to get the backing of the rulers in England for his edicts. It was a dark day in the history of the English Church when at the Synod of Whitby in 664 the King of Northumbria heard the differences between the leaders of the two churches and decided in favor of Rome. From that day until the time of John Wycliffe, centuries later, the Bible remained a Latin book and closed for the common people's understanding. Thereafter only wandering bards recited Biblical stories and ballads in English, by memory; thus in another way were the seven sons (the Church) changed into seven ravens and Israel began to look for a means of changing the ravens back into her fine brothers.

The search of Israel for her seven brothers is part of the inner urge of Israel, when she broke the bondage of Assyria and passed north and west beyond the headwaters of the Euphrates (as described in II Esdras) to eventually arrive in England. This journey is unrecorded in the **general** annals of History, and according to God's will was meant to be so.

In the story, the little daughter searched even to the sun, the moon and stars for her brothers, and all to no avail. The sun, the moon and the stars are symbols, identical here with those of Rev. 8:12.

"And the fourth angel sounded, and the third part of the sun was smitten, and the third part of the moon, and the third part of the stars." The sun, the moon and earth are symbols for the ruling powers of the earth, and in this passage of Revelation refer to Rome and the Roman governors in the provinces of the Roman empire. Not from earthly rulers was Israel to find any satisfaction in the search for her destiny, but finally, from one star (the young daughter of our story) found help. "But the morning star arose, and gave her the drumstick of a chicken, and said, 'If thou has not that drumstick thou canst not open the Glass Mountain, and in the Glass Mountain are thy brothers.''

Here we find three important symbols used, each of which is vital to the understanding of our story as it pertains to Israel. First, let us consider "the morning star", in contrast with the other stars mentioned previously. In Rev. 22:16 we have the statement from Jesus himself, "I Jesus, have sent mine angel to testify unto you these things in the churches. I am the root and the offspring of David, and the bright and **morning star**." There is no room for doubt here; the "morning star" is the same symbol of the Bible used by Jesus to describe himself, and is employed thusly in our story. In the next verse from the quotation given above, we are given an inkling of the role of Israel as relates to the Church: "And the Spirit and the **bride** (Israel) say, Come. And let him that heareth (the Overcomer) say, Come. And let him that is athirst, Come..." Israel, has a very distinct part to play in that great day when Christ shall come in His great glory and claim His bride as His own. Likewise, Israel plays a hidden but no less important role today as she who searches out all who might be readied as guests of the Bridegroom, when He comes.

What of the "drumstick" held out to the youngest daughter by the "morning star"? In the 14th verse of this same chapter in Revelation we read, "Blessed are they that do his commandments..." The "drumstick" is the fairy-story symbol for the commandments of God, graven upon the tablets of stone. The implication is that if Israel should keep the covenant and live according to God's will, she should enjoy the blessings of the Kingdom of Heaven upon earth. The symbol given in Daniel for this kingdom, as elsewhere, is a **"mountain."** In Daniel 2:35 this kingdom is described as the fifth and final kingdom which shall rule the earth: "and the stone that smote the image became a **great mountain**, filled the whole earth." In our story the "morning star" (Jesus) directs the young daughter (Israel) to the Glass Mountain as the place where she will find her brothers, but she is told she cannot get in without the "drumstick," i.e., she cannot have the kingdom without keeping God's laws.

Jesus in His ministry said, "think not that I am come to destroy the law, or the prophets: I am not come to destroy, but to fulfill." (Matthew 4:17) The covenant name of God, I AM, is also the name of the Christ. Moses was told to say to the children of Israel, "I AM hath sent me unto you." (Exodus 3:14). Had the temple priests and the Pharasees of Jerusalem recognized Jesus, the Christ, as the I AM" that sent Moses to lead the children of Israel, their acceptance of Him as the Messiah would have been more likely. When these argumentors harkened back to Abraham as their chief authority, Jesus answered them, "Before Abraham was, **I AM!**" again asserting his unity with the Godhead and announcing His identity. (John 8:58) Jesus gave His inner name publicly and privately in countless affirmations of His authority, such as "**I am** the bread of life," "**I am** the light of the world," "**I am** one that beareth witness of myself, and the Father that sent me beareth witness of me," "**I am** the door..." "**I am** the good shepherd," "**I am** the resurrection and the life." These are the few of many announcements of Jesus that He was and is the "I AM" that instructed Moses in the beginning and sought to lead His flock into the paths of righteousness, which should give them freedom and happiness. Men were blind to his true nature in that day; they are blind to His true nature today. Is it any wonder that He stated that He had come to fulfill the law, rather than to destroy it, He who had in His divine wisdom given forth the law? If today Christians realized that the laws of Israel were actually the laws of Jesus Christ would they not more seriously try to live by these laws? The time is very short when Jesus shall come and stand before the whole world and say "I Am come in judgement," just as He said in Jerusalem nearly two thousand years ago, but this time He shall come in power and glory. Men shall not crucify Him again, but rather shall He judge them by their faith or by their sins, and take to Himself His own.

"The maiden took the drumstick, wrapped it carefully in a cloth, and went onwards again until she came to the Glass Mountain. The door was shut, and she thought she would take out the drumstick, but when she undid the cloth, it was empty, and she had lost the good star's present. This loss of the drumstick is symbolic of the breaking of the covenant by the children of Israel and the loss of the lands of Canaan which God had given them. This passage is the subject-matter of the Book of Jeremiah in the Bible and the fulfillment of Jeremiah's prophecy is the destruction of Jerusalem and the capture of the House of Judah, similar to that of the House of Israel, and their removal as bond-slaves to the lands of Babylon. The kingdom of God became an unfulfilled promise to them, but only because of their rejection of God's laws and wishes for them.

The redemption of these people is next described in our story, the same redemption as depicted in the Bible, through the crucifixion of Jesus Christ. Having lost the drumstick (the covenant relationship having been broken) the "little sister took a knife, cut off one of her little fingers, put it in the door, and succeeded in opening it."

The "little finger" mentioned here is the symbol for Jesus Christ, and the "cutting off of the little finger" betokens the broken, bleeding body of our Lord upon the cross. It was by the willing sacrifice of Jesus that the sins and errors of Israel were cancelled out, so that she might go on to fulfill her destiny ordained of God. As a rescuer of Israel, Jesus clearly forsaw need of an intermediary agent, and that agent was himself. But the rescue will not be completed until the return of Jesus Himself to the earth, and at that time will Israel receive her promised reward. For let us not forget that Jesus is "he that is holy, he that is true, he that hath the key of David" (Rev. 3:7) and that as the Lion of Judah Jesus is, and will be, the king of all Israel, upon His return. The black cloak that enshrouds the Church today will not be removed until that great day; it shall be replaced at that time with a garment of shining white light, even the "garment of righteousness" which is ready to be worn by the saints.

Jesus left with His disciples the simple ceremony of the Holy Communion to remind them of His sacrifice. "And he took bread, and gave thanks, and brake it, and gave unto them, saying, This is my body which is given for you: this do in remembrance of me." (Luke 22:19) Jesus saw the importance of Christians down through the centuries to remind themselves of His sacrifice. It is through the observance of this request of His that Christians draw closer to each other in love and are prompted to follow in the Way of the Master.

By means of the Christ shall Israel have her inheritance and enter into the rewards of the Kingdom and through her shall the Church be rescued from the spell that has been cast upon her. As the two witnesses shall they stand side by side before the God of the earth and perceive His glory and His great benificence. And so, in our story, it is by means of her little finger that the maiden opens the door into the Glass Mountain. Having gained entry into the mountain the seven ravens are not to be found too readily. We here get an insight into the manner in which the seven brothers (the church) are to be restored. A dwarf shows the maiden where the ravens were want to stay, but tells her that they are not at home, "The lord ravens are not at home, but if you will wait here until they come, step in."

As the dwarf brings in dinner in preparation for the coming of the ravens we see the maid tasting of each plate, and sipping from each glass. "In the last glass she dropped a ring which she had brought away with her." It is significant here that it is the maid (Israel) who has the ring and that it is by recognizing this ring that the ravens knew their little sister and are magically changed back into their human form again. Thereupon they embraced and kissed each other and went joyfully home."

The transformation of the ravens into the seven brothers is described in Rev. 11:12: "the Spirit of the life of God entered into them, and they stood upon their feet; and great fear fell upon them which saw them. And they heard a great voice from heaven saying unto them, Come up hither. And they ascended up to heaven in a cloud, and their enemies beheld them." The transformation of Israel and the Church will actually take place at the same time: the glorified Church and sanctified Israel will rise together in the ascension. Thus, the pattern which Jesus set for them on the hill of Bethany so long ago, will take effect for thousands of individuals in the very near future. It remains for those of the Church to look upon "the ring" that will identify Israel for them, and then shall they rejoice and return home with her to the Father. This process of revealing the marks of identification of Israel is now in progress, and it is imperative that as many as possible in the Church awaken to this great truth. It is essential to their own salvation as well as national Israel. It is not destined for all in the Church to awaken, as indicated in Matthew 25:1, but joyous rewards await those who do. Discernment and decision: these are the two qualities which Jesus would ask of his followers in these turbulent days. And there are two other words which He left for those of this generation which we should honor, "watch and pray!"

Again, in the story of the Seven Ravens we have been given a pattern of the past and a pattern for the future. We note that this story, as do the other Saxon tales, has an assuring note of certainty for us, today. The story backs up the Bible. It opens our eyes as to the meaning of the second and third chapters of Revelation, which is an enigma to many. It is a story for children, yes, but only secondarily so. It was designed to strengthen the wavering Christian of today, to reveal to him the times in which he lives in a new light, and so extend to him courage and promise for the future. Marvelous events lie just ahead for him, could he but see them. It is for this purpose that the Saxon folk-tales were created. They were meant to entertain children, yes, but further than that, they were to strengthen the faith of the believer and enlarge his understanding, that he might be a more vibrant Christian, faithful, true and strong.

THE END

APPENDIX

THE STRANGEST ALIAS IN HISTORY

Many reasons and motives have prompted men to assume other names. Circumstances have arisen which, for the sake of protection, have called for an alias. The hiding of a man's identity beneath an assumed name has enabled him to pass unnoticed where recognition would have involved peril. One of the most difficult tasks of police authorities is to strip a suspected person of any aliases under which he or she may have been living in order to disclose the individual's true identity. Men have mysteriously disappeared from their frequented environments by the simple device of changing their names. Memory is short and a person is soon forgotten, although he may be still living in very close proximity to his former surroundings. Thus, the use of an alias is an extremely effective means of obscuring identity.

A Whole Race Disappears

Only once in human history, with its multitudinous vagaries, has it been recorded that a whole race completely disappeared from sight, seeming to leave no trace behind it. So completely was its identity obliterated that, although still in existence and better known to the whole world than any of its contemporaries, the nations comprising it having a foremost place in history and envied by those striving for world dominion, it still passes unrecognized by the world generally as to its true identity. A commonwealth of nations and a great nation living under an alias! Truth is often stranger than fiction and it would need the pen of a genius and the imagination of some great writer to vividly depict and weave into story form this hiding of nations and the obscuring of their identity while they unobtrusively play the greatest role that has even been the lot of any race in the unfolding drama of human relationships.

How comparatively few who read the best-known Book in the world have discovered in it this strange story. How comparatively few have realized that the Bible contains a story thread at all, much less that it is the story of the people created by Almighty God for world service, with a Divine pledge of imperishability, destined at the end of its long journey to lead the nations of the world into the Kingdom of God on earth and to consummate the Divine purpose of blessing every family of the human race. The nations formed by that people are to become the focal center of world destiny upon which the eyes of the whole world look and to which they turn for guidance, help and deliverance - yet all the while their true identity is unrecognized. This is no mere fiction; it is actual truth and fact. With cynical smile, scoffing word or impatient, incredulous gesture, men dismiss as the fad of

121

a fanatic or the warped idea of a crank the suggestion that, in spite of all their boasted sagacity, they have failed to identify the best-known nations in the world. But so it was intended. How perfectly the alias hides its secret! How completely the identity remains obscured!

The Reason for the Alias

Surely there must be a reason - an important reason - for this remarkable alias? Surely behind what it conceals there must be a Master Mind? It is that reason and that Master Mind which make the story live. How thrilling it must be to pass unnoticed while rubbing shoulders with one's fellows, listening to what they say about one, sharing with them things held in common, all the time wondering at their blindness in failing to see the obvious. And more so since a part of the story in the Bible offers a minute description of the people in question, a vivid word picture so clear in detail that, once attention is drawn to it, one wonders how it could ever have been missed.

It is like the hidden figure intertwined in some drawing which challenges us to find it. How we look and turn the drawing about from side to side, upside down and at every angle. But once it has been found, it stares out at us every time we look at it and we wonder how it could have been possible not to see it before. So it is with the national alias. The national instruments for world blessing march down their prescribed avenues of world history to do a work they could not have done were it universally known who they really are.

The Missed Story of the Bible

Because the story of the Bible has been missed, the story of the alias has been overlooked as well. How hard it is to wean ourselves away from traditional beliefs and the confused vocabulary by which men endeavor to interpret the Scriptures. Accepted theology has obscured perfectly plain meanings and common sense has become confused by involved explanations and complicated exegeses. Why not call a spade a spade; why not believe that God means what He says and says what He means in intelligible language. God has planned it that His purposes shall be perfectly clear to all so that "the wayfaring men, though fools, shall not err therein" (Isa. 35:8). When He uses a symbol, He so states. When He employs figurative language, it is obvious. When He speaks in terms of literal history or narrative, He means it to be taken as such. It is this confusing of vital issues which has caused the ordinary reader to miss the story of the Bible. He has been made afraid to take things literally and, when he has had the courage to do so, the Church has resented his action as an infringement of its prerogative to interpret.

A People hidden for 2,520 Years

The strangest alias of history is written in terms of simple, everyday language. For over 2,520 years God has had a people in the world living under an alias. It is only now, in the days in which you and I live, that the identity of the people so hidden is due to be revealed. The specified time period of the alias is terminating. The time for the greatest discovery of history is at hand. Slowly but surely world events are lifting the veil and disclosing the origin and the identity of what has for so long been the greatest enigma of human happening.

Let us await God's time; it is not for us to run before history, however eager we may be to make the facts known. To allow our impatience to anticipate God is to betray an ignorance of the Divine purpose or a failure to trust Him to do in His own way and time what He has promised to do. It is not for us to play the role of the private detective, but rather to watch with deepening interest and wonderment how He is carrying through His design. We may often have wondered why our well-meant efforts in public and in private to explain the alias have met with, to us, an inexplicable countermove that has frustrated our efforts. Is it not the evident sign that we have been premature in our eagerness to hurry things? To force open a door so carefully kept closed before the opening time is to hinder rather than help.

"He that believeth shall not make haste." Yet it is the very thing we, in our earnestness, wish most of all to do. Why won't people listen? Why can't they see? Some have even wanted a national proclamation to be issued, identifying the Anglo-Saxon-Celtic peoples with Israel of old, or have deplored the fact that the Christian Church cannot be compelled to see the truth so as to make an official declaration concerning the true identity of present-day Israel.

Why all this haste? Can we not trust God to do in His own time what, after all, concerns Him far more vitally than it can ever concern us? Shall we try to remember that not all have seen the hidden figure in the drawing - that they do not see what you or I may have discovered. May I urge you to bear with a word of exhortation? It is not our task to remove the national alias, however eager or earnest we may be to disclose the identity beneath it. Shall we try to understand that those closed doors, that opposition, that refusal or apparent unwillingness to listen, may be the very way, perhaps the only way, by which God is able to curb our impetuosity and so prevent our spoiling His plan?

This thing is too big, too world significant, too far-reaching to be rendered ineffective by well-meaning but mistaken human interference. World destiny is wrapped up in this alias. How lovingly God deals with us and our deep desire to help Him, but how often He must smile at our childlike lack of understanding while appreciating the motive that would persist in premature action. We want to move forward now — and He has waited patiently for 2,520 years for the very same thing !

Why the Alias Still Remains

What lies hidden beneath this alias? Why is it such a zealously-guarded secret? Sufficient information has already been revealed to let us know that the British Commonwealth of free nations and the great people of the United States of America are no ordinary nations among the peoples of the world; that they are there for world service, for the uplift of mankind, for the maintenance of law and order and the establishment of the basic principles of righteousness, justice and freedom in the earth. With no uncertain voice the Holy Scriptures declare that the alias - the change of name - was given to the House of Jacob, the descendants of Abraham, Isaac and Jacob. That was the Divinely-appointed line through which blessing was to reach all mankind, the people called in the New Testament "the Commonwealth of Israel."

Make no mistake here, for this alias has nothing to do with the Jew of history. The Bible most plainly records that neither Abraham, nor Isaac, nor Jacob were Jews. Never has it been necessary or desired to change the name of the Jew. Nothing has ever hidden the identity of the Jew.

On the other hand, you know the story of Jacob, that moment in his career when he met God and wrestled with the Angel. It was the supreme crisis in his life and experience when his name was changed from Jacob to Israel. With a changed life and character he was to rule with God. The nations that came from him to play their great part in the world drama have to graduate in the same school. As he wrestled and prevailed, so must the Anglo-Saxon nations wrestle and prevail until their name, too, may be changed and the alias under which they have traveled down their predestined roads gives place to the name by which all shall know that they, too, rule with God for their blessing and for His glory.

Today we are passing through the time of national Jacob's trouble, which is leading us out into the time of renewal, readiness and worthiness to receive the new name, that of Israel. We are facing our Peniel in this welter of tribulation and tears in order that we, like Jacob, may learn to depend utterly upon God alone; that we, like Jacob, may realize that we dare not let God go until He blesses us. When that day dawns, God will be able to trust us with that name of which He is a part, Isra-el (ruling with God).

The identity is all right; nothing changes that. That has never been in question. The main issue is, When shall we be able to have it made known that we have prevailed with God, taken our place on His side, forsaken our old evil ways, and have been changed and renewed? Then, and only then, will the world know "whose we are and whom we serve."

Must we cease, then, to proclaim our identity? Why should we? It is part of the Divine plan; part of the Bible story. We must continue to proclaim it so that those who have eyes to see and ears to hear may see and hear, although the majority remain in ignorance. But let us proclaim it in its right setting - proclaim the struggle that will bring the nation out of the night into the day as we pass over and out of the old life into the new, no more Jacob, but Israel. Then will the strangest alias of all history yield its long-guarded secret and the whole world will rejoice. Thereupon, triumphant voices will be raised in exaltation: "Arise, shine; for thy light is come, and the glory of the Lord is risen upon thee. . . . And the Gentiles shall come to thy light, and kings to the brightness of thy rising." (Isa. 60:1-3)

(Rev.) Claud Coffin

THE ILLUSTRATIONS

Countless illustrations have been made for the many volumes of the "Household Tales" gathered by the Brothers Grimm in Hesse. The stories have been translated into many languages with each volume embellished with a new sheaf of illustrations. The story of Snow-white and the Seven Dwarfs was made into a cartoon-type motion picture by Walt Disney which has been enjoyed by several generations of children all around the world. The picture is one of the most widely viewed in the history of the motion picture industry and is still being shown periodically. The illustrations in this book have been done by the author in pen-and-ink as he made forays into "the Land of Once Upon a Time" and visited the places in Hesse associated with the stories, beginning in 1956. Since that time there has been a growing awareness of the importance of these places as they mark the unfolding of the Fairy Tale past. A general effort to preserve the old Post-and-Beam structures along what is now called "The Fairy Tale Street" is in progress and visitors can be grateful for this splendid program of preservation of these buildings. The very house where Dorothea Thiehmann lived near Cassel has been restored, one room of which holds the original furniture which she used when she lived there... perhaps even the chairs upon which the Grimm Brothers sat when they came to audit the stories which she told them.

The acknowledged route of the Fairy Tale Street today stretches from Hanau, where the Grimm brothers were born, to Bremen, where an iron statue has been erected in the town plaza to the "Bremen Town-Musicians", with a rooster, a hound and a cat all miraculously poised on the back of a donkey. In the very center of this Fairy Tale country is the Meissner, a heavily wooded mountain rising in the Werra Land, offering a magnificent view of the surrounding countryside. Frau Holle Lake lies near the top of this huge land mass, which doubtless furnished fresh water and refuge to many of the tribes of Israel as they traveled to their new countries "north and west." There is an aura of mystic reverence attached to this place, all gathered about the person of Frau Holle, one of the most beloved of the Fairy Tale figures. She might well be another symbol for Israel, as suggested by the description of the woman in Revelations 12 of the Bible. The spirit of Frau Holle pervades the region of the Meissner where she continues to reign as the Queen Mother of all the other fairyland figures.

These latter-day illustrations are included to add a sense of reality to the reading of the Fairy stories, as one explores the ancient past of the splendid and honorable people God named "Israel." In many ways the passage of the tribes of Israel from Assyria northwest through the forests of Europe can be retraced, but none so easily as by the Post-and-Beam method of building which they developed, and which are herein depicted.

LIST OF ILLUSTRATIONS

1. The house where Dorothea Viehmann, "The Fairy Tale Wife," lived in Niederzwehren, a village near Cassel, Germany. The Brothers Grimm visited her here, adding more than twenty new tales to their collection. She died in 1815, only a year after the publication of the second volume of "The Household Tales."

2. The old tower, originally marking the entrance to the once walled town of Eschwege, still stands today, a silent sentinal of the past. The wall has long since disappeared, the stones being used to build houses.

   Eschwege was the locale for the story of the "Shoemaker and the Elves". It is here that the shoemaker lived and worked and one night was helped by a bevy of the "little people" who inhabited the area. Visiting Eschwege today it is easy to imagine the presence of these tiny helpers of the fabled shoemaker of Eschwege.

3. In the old plaza of Eschwege stands St. Katherine's Church, a 15th century Gothic structure still in use. It survived the Peasant's Revolt in 1525 when all of the stained glass windows were broken out, crucifixed destroyed and all statues were thrown into the

127

Werra River. Plain glass replaced the stained glass. Only the ornate pulpit was retained.

Eschwege was founded in 715 as a Frankish kingdom. In the 10th century it came into the hands of the Saxon kings. About the middle of the 12th century Eschwege received state's rights and was a free city until the 13th century. In 1433 it came into the possession of Hessen. High above the city is seen the castle of the Dukes of Hessen. The market place is surrounded by well-kept Post-and-Beam houses, a sign of the presence of the "sons of Isaac," (Saxons). On the edge of the plaza can be found the Town Hall dated 1660. On another side stands the church of St. Dionys, its western turret going back to the 13th century. Ruins of the old cloister of St. Cyriax can be found close by.

4. The ancient castle and town of Runtel on the Lahn.

5. The magestic castle of Marksburg by the Braubach.

6. A manor house at Wanfried, showing the carriage house and entry. Wanfried is within view of the Eastern Zone.

7. Friedberg Castle in Hesse, where Rapunzel might well have lived.

8. Some fine old Saxon post-and-beam structures at Bad Sooden, backed by the high tower of St. Marienkirche and wooded hills.

9. The unique Town Hall at Bad Sooden, with the cobbled street running through the building and under the tower. The building on the right is the Pfenig House, where the salt was measured out from a heavy stone table and sold by the penny.

10. An intricate design achieved in Saxon Post-and-Beam fashion on the side of one of the cobbled streets of Bad Sooden.

11. Across the River Werra from Bad Sooden is the companion town of Allendorf, meaning a "town for all people."

12. The bell tower of Allendorf church rises above the tiled roof tops of Allendorf.

13. The beam-patterned walls of the town hall rises on one side of the marketplatz in Allendorf. The fountain shows the four elements, with element of fire depicted on the one water spout.

14. On the main street of Allendorf, Hessen.

15. Hofgeismar-Sababurg, called "the Sleeping Beauty Castle" is nestled among the trees near Cassel, suggesting the high hedge of the Fairy Tale.

16. A cottage in Welford-on-Avon, a few miles from Stratford-on-Avon, in England. The migrations of the Saxons ("Isaac's sons) through Europe to Britain can to traced by the Post-and-Beam construction of the houses.

James Haggart '80

1

2

James Haggart 1936
Neustädter Kirche-Eschwege

3

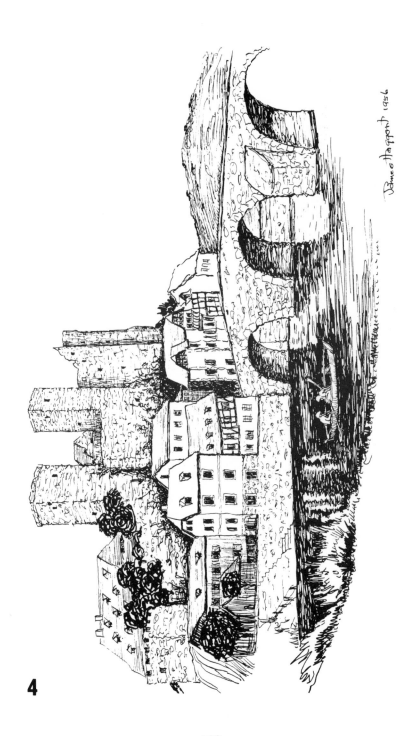

4

5

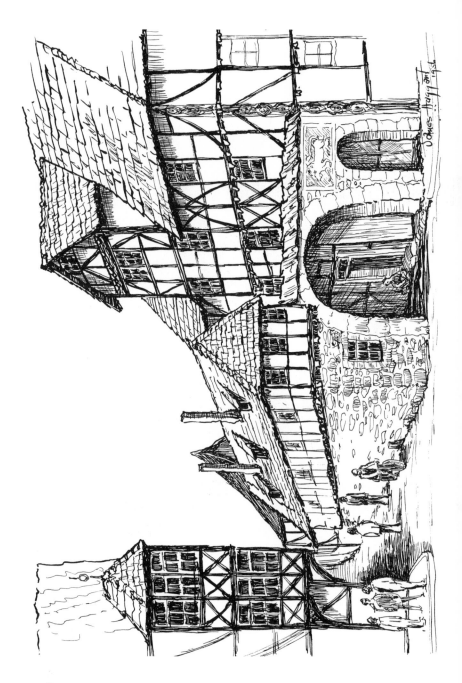

6

James Haggart
1956

7

8

9

10

James Haggart 1956

11

James Haggart '80

12

James Haggart '80

13

14

James Haggart '80

15

16